PROUST'S BINOCULARS

PROUST'S BINOCULARS

A Study of Memory, Time,
and Recognition
in
A la recherche du temps perdu

———◆———

ROGER
SHATTUCK

PRINCETON UNIVERSITY PRESS
PRINCETON, NEW JERSEY

Published by Princeton University Press,
41 William Street, Princeton, New Jersey 08540

Copyright © 1962, 1983 by Roger Shattuck
All rights reserved

First edition, Alfred A. Knopf, 1963
First Vintage Books edition, 1967
First Princeton Paperback printing, 1983

LCC 82-48567
ISBN 0-691-01403-5 pbk.

Quotations from Proust's works are copyrighted and reprinted by Random House, Inc., and Editions Gallimard.

Clothbound editions of Princeton University Press books are printed on acid-free paper, and binding materials are chosen for strength and durability. Paperbacks, while satisfactory for personal collections, are not usually suitable for library rebinding.

Printed in the United States of America by Princeton University Press, Princeton, New Jersey

CONTENTS

PROUST'S BINOCULARS

I

Out of the vastness of his literary wisdom and the extensiveness of his literary work, Proust himself made most of the relevant comments on his own writings. Like the Bible, *A la recherche du temps perdu* embodies its own sources, myths, and criticism. It comes to stand for a state of civilization. Yet Proust's excavation of his particular world through the artistic process became so rich in detail that we often fail to discern what he was digging for and what he found. Thus one understands why the "meaning" of Proust, the nature of his esthetic approach to life, has rarely been articulated outside his own work. And the difficulty of Proust has another aspect too easily overlooked: what he says intimately concerns our consciousness of ourselves as human beings faced with the appalling responsibility of living our lives. Challenged both to understand and to act accordingly, we tend to neglect his true meaning for peripheral and exotic parts of his work. We should not tolerate so great a loss.

To read Proust is like looking at a map on which one sees clearly the names of all the cities and rivers and principal provinces, but not the name of the country itself; and not until much later, when one's eyes have finally relaxed, renouncing the possibility of ever discovering that information on the map, does one suddenly perceive, large as life and as if by chance, the name written in bold letters over the entire surface of the area; and then that name, which was so hard to see when one was looking right at it, turns out to be not unknown but only forgotten—one of the places read about in childhood and associated with miraculous trees bearing bread and dates, and animals with monstrous but very useful tails and noses, yet a country never visited and rarely mentioned in the everyday version of the world's events. Proust's "meaning" is written thus in capitals across his entire work, yet most readers give up without having found it. It is a marvelous testimony to his genius for fleshing out his universe that such readers are usually satisfied with what they carry away. The fact that they may not know where they have been rarely dampens their enthusiasm.[1]

My entry into Proust's country is provided by one of his most celebrated passages on style. It concludes:[2]

. . . la vérité ne commencera qu'au moment
où l'écrivain . . . en rapprochant une qualité
commune à deux sensations, dégagera leur essence commune en les réunissant l'une et l'autre pour les soustraire aux contingences du
temps, dans une métaphore. (III 889)

. . . truth will begin only when the writer . . . comparing similar qualities in two
sensations, makes their essential nature stand
out clearly by joining them, in order to remove
them from the contingencies of time, in a metaphor. (II 1008-1009)

(Metaphor here means all types of figurative discourse.) The variety and power and significance of
Proust's images have often been studied, yet very
few of them have been tracked to their source and
revealed in their full significance. The two portions
of the world he invoked most frequently to yield
comparisons are the realm of art and the realm of
science. The two great illusory values in the book,
the sentiment of love and the prestige of nobility,
crystallize and dissolve in a solution of images based
on music and painting; the great transformations of
social upheaval and old age at the end are set before us in terms of zoology. And like Homer,
Proust is full of images of eating and culinary en-
joyment, as if the surest way of knowing a thing
is to eat it, or at least to pick it up and smell it.
Yet there is a further class of images, partaking of
both art and science, which gradually reveals itself
as significant in a particular manner.

The first objects distinct from the *I* mentioned in A *la recherche* appear in the second sentence: Marcel's candle and his eyes. On the following page his lengthy reveries on the verge of sleep are condensed into the image of "the kaleidoscope of darkness"; six pages later the first familiar object seized and described out of his childhood world of Combray turns out to be a magic lantern; it entertains Marcel by transforming his bedroom into a series of legendary and historical scenes. This strand of imagery, linking not so much things seen as particular circumstances or modes of vision, never slackens through three thousand pages of text. Thus we should reach the final figure in the book prepared to understand its composite meaning. The "stilts" on which a man sways dizzily in old age represent not only the precariousness of his life and the awkwardness of his movements but also the perspective of his mind, the lofty vantage point from which he views the world. The point is worth belaboring. Proust drew on an incredibly rich repertory of metaphors. But it is principally through the science and the art of *optics* that he beholds and depicts the world. Truth—and Proust believed in it—is a miracle of vision.

A systematic cataloguing of visual figures reveals a great deal in a short space. The simplest optical imagery results from the particular attention Proust pays to visual and light effects, most of them in nature, a few of them associated with art. The description in the early pages of the novel of the setting sun lighting only the upper portion of the

steeple of Saint Hilaire (1 64/1 48), prepares the way
for a similar view of obliquely illuminated trees in
the last volume. The stained-glass windows of the
same church seem to come to life in the play of
sunlight—or perhaps it is only the movement of
Marcel's glance (1 59-60/1 45-46). At the sea resort
of Balbec, the beauty and fascination of the ocean
consists in the "diversity of its lighting" (1 673/
1 511). Marcel speaks of the room of his friend,
Saint-Loup, in Doncières as an "optical center"
(II 81/I 771) because of its excellent view of the
hillside. The range of sensations afforded by the
sight of Venice suggests the idea of an "optical
pedal" (II 146/I 818-819). In his imagination Marcel sees the row of holy days at Easter as if touched
by a special light (II 143/I 817). Less through
lengthy description than through vivid highlighting,
Marcel's world is rendered visually.

The further one advances into the work, the
richer the optical imagery becomes. To refine and
intensify the visual effects in nature, Proust un-
limbers a whole set of optical instruments to accom-
pany the kaleidoscope and magic-lantern figures of
the opening pages, often reused. In one of his
earliest stories, Proust spoke of a character's "double
reputation" as a "deceptive prism through which
each person tried to distinguish his true traits" (*Les
Plaisirs et les jours*, p. 166). The magic aura of
Balbec lingers in Marcel's mind as if he could see it
"in the magnifying lens of one of those fountain
pens for sale at beach resorts" (1 389/1 297). The
monocle, described at length in all its comic varieties,

becomes one of the principal attributes of a whole
set of characters among the nobility (I 326-7, 729/
I 250-1, 552; III 953, 984/——, ——). At the crucial
moment of the scene in which Marcel kisses Albertine—it is the only such description in the book—
Proust abruptly veers off into what appears to be
a digression on "the latest applications of photography" that reveal the face of the earth in new perspective. Yet he is only closing in on his subject: "I
see only this [photography] which can, to so great
a degree as a kiss, summon forth out of what we
may believe to be the definite aspect of a thing the
hundred other things which it is just as well, for
each is related to a perspective no less legitimate"
(II 365/I 979). The same photographic imagery and
vocabulary give an intensely visual cast to the celebrated scene of Marcel's walking in on his grandmother when she does not expect him and suddenly
beholding her as an old woman, a stranger whom he
does not recognize (II 140-41/I 814-815). And it is
for his grandmother that the act of being photo-
graphed by Saint-Loup assumes momentous proportions (I 786-88, II 776-77/I 593-596, II 127-128). In
the last volume, the comparison of a writer seeking
psychological laws to a surgeon seeking the seat
of a disease condenses into an optical image of the
artist who "fluoroscopes" what he sees (III 719/
II 888).

A further set of optical images also effects
changes in perspective or point of view, but without
the use of an optical instrument other than our own
consciousness—the most sensitive of all. Marcel

speaks of "the general laws which govern perspective in the imagination" (II 235/I 884). In the opening volume the key incident associated with the steeples of Martinville rests on the visual experience of Marcel's seeing from a moving carriage three church steeples in rapidly shifting perspective. The painter Elstir exploits the same effect of disturbed or confused vision: "The attempt to show things not as he knew they were but according to these optical illusions out of which our primary vision is made, led him . . . to illuminate certain of these laws of perspective" (I 838/I 630-631, cf. II 419/I 1018). One of the best passages to illustrate the optical illusion of our perception of the world comes at the very end of Swann's protracted and agonizing love affair with Odette. He sees her for the last time in a dream which ends with the tolling of a bell and the spectacle of a city in flames. Swann's servant wakes him, saying it is eight o'clock and the barber has arrived. "But these words, penetrating into the depths of sleep where Swann was plunged, had reached his consciousness only after undergoing that deviation which makes a ray of light appear under water as a sun, just as a moment before the sound of the bell, in taking on in the depths the sonority of a curfew, had given birth to the incident of the fire" (I 380/I 291). This passage, coming as it does just as Swann begins to recover from his love in the closing pages of the section, presents itself as a figure not only for his dream, but for the entire love affair in which he was submerged as in a new medium. Every sensation penetrated his consciousness on a bias. More even than the dream, his love has been an optical illusion to which he has devoted several years of his life.

It is not merely the number and vividness of these optical images that indicate their importance in Proust's work. They occur at the most strategic places and illuminate values central to the development of the action. The social ordering of the novel will bring this out most readily. At first the social classes appear to Marcel and to the reader as clearly defined layers; and, of necessity, perception from one level to the next, or to a level several times removed, entails severe refraction and distortion. Marcel, looking up toward the higher circles, misjudges everyone in the beginning. This distortion in social depth perception is described occurring in the opposite direction in the scene where the Princesse de Luxembourg, from the altitude of her nobility, tries to be gracious on meeting Marcel and his grandmother. "And, even, in her desire not to appear to hold forth from a sphere superior to ours, she had miscalculated the distance, for, by an error in adjustment, her looks were filled with so great a kindness I foresaw the moment when she would pet us like two lovable animals who had stretched out our necks toward her through the grillwork at the Jardin d'Acclimatation" (1 699/1 530). This miscalculation of station is brief and trivial compared to the complex stages of Marcel's attitude toward the Guermantes. Out of his youthful admiration for the Duchesse de Guermantes—a sentiment copied in him like a "magic-lantern slide and a stained-glass window" (II 11/I 720)—grows the "artificial enlargement" (II 568/I 1121-2) of his image of that whole clan. It engulfs him. Gradually these simple images of distorted perception yield to figures which contain an expression of social mobility—above all the famous "social kaleidoscope" (II 190/I 851, III 893/II 1012). The social levels lose their hierarchy, and by the end we lose sight even of the two *côtés* whose originally opposed perspectives are fragmented and crossed in both social and subjective upheaval.

The individual order of love suffers, or benefits, from comparable distortions, as has already been brought out in the passage on Swann's dream. Having spoken in his preface to Ruskin's *Sésame et les lys* of "the optics of minds" (p. 32) which prevents us from absorbing knowledge from others, Proust goes on to write of the "infra-red" by which Marcel perceives Gilberte's secret qualities (I 416/ I 317) and of "those two equally distorting optics" (I 587/I 447) of his love for her which he could not reconcile. Finally comes this description of the women we love: "Those women are a product of our temperament, an image, a reversed projection, a 'negative' of our sensibility" (I 894/I 671). Even more than love, jealousy is victimized by twisted perspective, and Marcel wonders "by what optical illusion" (III 190/II 511) he missed seeing some minor detail about Albertine, "for the world of stars is less difficult to know than the real actions of people." And just as we witness two different versions of Rachel, as seen by her lover Saint-Loup and by the indifferent Marcel, we are finally offered two different versions of Albertine, as seen by the same two men with their roles reversed. Saint-Loup cannot believe that the photograph Marcel shows him is of the girl he has been talking about. The whole passage turns on the faculty of sight. After an inevitable astronomical reference to the illusory location of the sun, we read: "So difference in optic extends not only to people's physical appearance but to their character, and to their individual importance" (III 439/II 690). There was a time when Proust, like the romantics, believed that the eyes of lovers could pierce all media. "They looked into each others' eyes, revealing their souls along the edge of the pupils." (*Les Plaisirs et les jours*, p. 41; also p. 28.) The mysterious attraction of the Duchesse de Guermantes resides ultimately in her *regard*, carefully described both in the church at Combray and in her *baignoire* at the Opera. But the eye loses its powers of revelation for Marcel, and neither Albertine nor Charlus are capable of looking at anyone directly. Before the shiftiness of their look, he is thrown back upon an inner optics, an investigation of subjective states.

Sleep, memory, imagination, sense of identity —here are indeed the basic areas of refraction and illusion, and Proust allows his optical imagery to crystallize around these crucial mental operations. Rather than accumulating several examples of how Proust proceeds in these cases, I shall quote one lengthy passage to indicate the central role of optical imagery as he used it, and the extent to which

he adapts it both to social and subjective spheres.
Attending his first important social gathering, the
matinée chez Mme. de Villeparisis, Marcel has been
particularly amazed by the unreliability of our relations with people and by the "mobility" of their
opinion of us. He learns that M. de Norpois, who
always appeared to have a benevolent attitude toward him, has called him a "semi-hysterical flat-
terer." I quote the following paragraph in its entirety.

J'ai raconté bien auparavant ma stupéfaction
qu'un ami de mon père comme était M. de
Norpois eût pu s'exprimer ainsi en parlant de
moi. J'en éprouvai une plus grande encore à
savoir que mon émoi de ce jour ancien où
j'avais parlé de Mme. Swann et de Gilberte
était connu par la princesse de Guermantes de
qui je me croyais ignoré. Chacune de nos actions, de nos paroles, de nos attitudes est
séparée du "monde," des gens qui ne l'ont pas
directement perçue, par un milieu dont la per-
méabilité varie à l'infini et nous reste inconnue.
Ayant appris par l'expérience que tel propos
important que nous avions souhaité vivement
être propagé (tels ceux si enthousiastes que je
tenais autrefois à tout le monde et en toute occasion sur Mme Swann, pensant que parmi
tant de bonnes graines répandues il s'en trou-
verait bien une qui lèverait) s'est trouvé, souvent à cause de notre désir même, immédiate-
ment mis sous le boisseau, combien à plus forte

raison étions-nous éloignés de croire que telle parole minuscule, oubliée de nous-mêmes, voire jamais prononcée par nous et formée en route par l'imparfaite réfraction d'une parole différente, serait transportée, sans que jamais sa marche s'arrêtât, à des distances infinies—en l'espèce jusque chez la princesse de Guermantes —et allât divertir à nos dépens le festin des dieux! Ce que nous nous reppelons de notre conduite reste ignoré de notre plus proche voisin; ce que nous avons oublié avoir dit, ou même ce que nous n'avons jamais dit, va provoquer l'hilarité jusque dans une autre planète, et l'image que les autres se font de nos faits et gestes ne ressemble pas plus à celle que nous nous en faisons nous-mêmes qu'à un dessin quelque décalque râté, où tantôt au trait noir correspondrait un espace vide, et à un blanc un contour inexplicable. Il peut du reste arriver que ce qui n'a pas été transcrit soit quelque trait irréel que nous ne voyons que par complaisance, et que ce qui nous semble ajouté nous appartienne au contraire, mais si essentiellement que cela nous échappe. De sorte que cette étrange épreuve qui nous semble si peu ressemblante a quelquefois le genre de vérité, peu flatteur certes, mais profond et utile, d'une photographie par les rayons X. Ce n'est pas une raison pour que nous nous y reconnaissions. Quelqu'un qui a l'habitude de sourire dans la glace à sa belle figure et à son beau torse, si on lui montre leur radiographie, aura devant ce chapelet osseux, indiqué comme étant une image de lui-même, le même soupçon d'une erreur que le visiteur d'une exposition qui, devant un portrait de jeune femme, lit dans le catalogue: "Dromadaire couché." Plus tard, cet écart entre notre image selon qu'elle est dessinée par nous-mêmes ou par autrui, je devais m'en rendre compte pour d'autres que moi, vivant béatement au milieu d'une collection de photographies qu'ils avaient tirées d'eux-mêmes tandis qu'alentour grimaçaient d'effroyables images, habituellement invisibles pour eux-mêmes, mais qui les plongeaient dans la stupeur si un hasard les leur montrait en leur disant: "C'est vous." (II 271-272)

I have recorded a long way back my stupefaction at the discovery that a friend of my father, such as M. de Norpois was, could have expressed himself thus in speaking of me. I was even more astonished to learn that my emotion on that evening long ago when I had asked him about Mme. Swann and Gilberte was known to the Princesse de Guermantes, whom I imagined never to have heard of my existence. Each of our actions, our words, our attitudes is cut off from the "world," from the people who have not directly perceived it, by a medium the permeability of which is of infinite variation and remains unknown to ourselves; having learned by experience that some important utterance which we eagerly hoped would be disseminated (such as those so enthusiastic speeches which I used at one time to make to all comers and on every occasion on the subject of Mme. Swann) has found itself, often simply on account of our anxiety, immediately hidden under a bushel, how immeasurably less do we suppose that some tiny word, which we ourselves have forgotten, or else a word never uttered by us but formed on its course by the imperfect refraction of a different word, can be transported without ever halting for any obstacle to infinite distances—in the present instance to the Princesse de Guermantes—and succeed in diverting at our expense the banquet of the gods. What we actually recall of our conduct remains unknown to our nearest neighbour; what we have forgotten that we ever said, or indeed what we never did say, flies to provoke hilarity even in another planet, and the image that other people form of our actions and behaviour is no more like that which we form of them ourselves, than is like an original drawing a spoiled copy in which, at one point, for a black line, we find an empty gap, and for a blank space an unaccountable contour. It may be, all the same, that what has not been transcribed is some non-existent feature which we behold merely in our purblind self-esteem, and that what seems to us added is indeed a part of ourselves, but so essential a part as to have escaped our notice. So that this strange

print which seems to us to have so little re-
semblance to ourselves bears sometimes the
same stamp of truth, scarcely flattering, indeed,
but profound and useful, as a photograph taken
by X-rays. Not that that is any reason why we
should recognise ourselves in it. A man who is
in the habit of smiling in the glass at his hand-
some face and stalwart figure, if you shew him
their radiograph, will have, face to face with
that rosary of bones, labelled as being the image
of himself, the same suspicion of error as the
visitor to an art gallery who, on coming to the
portrait of a girl, reads in his catalogue: "Drom-
edary resting." Later on, this discrepancy between our portraits, according as it was our own
hand that drew them or another, I was to
register in the case of others than myself, living placidly in the midst of a collection of
photographs which they themselves had taken
while round about them grinned frightful faces,
invisible to them as a rule, but plunging them
in stupor if an accident were to reveal them
with the warning: "This is you." (I 910-911)

The sequence of optical figures becomes clearer and
more precise as the paragraph opens out and then
closes, starting with the innocent word *milieu* and
carrying the general laws of optics into X-ray photography: *milieu, propage* (propagates), *réfraction,
image, épreuve* (proof), *photographie, radiographie,
tirées* (taken, drawn out, printed). This last word
is so ambiguous and so specific in its photographic

sense as to complement the superb comic and mimetic turn of the last sixteen lines. The progression from general optical laws to X-ray photography corresponds to the shift in theme from the confounding in society of acts, words, and attitudes (summed up in an astronomical image), to our inability to confront ourselves (expressed by the flimsy likeness of snapshots). The transition is made perfectly nakedly in the sentence beginning "It may be . . . ," which says that we can be mistaken as much about ourselves as about others.

Reserving other aspects of this paragraph for later consideration, I should like to insist here that its underlying theme of the inaccuracy of perception furnishes us with the first clue to the significance of all this optical imagery. The science of optics forever shows the *errors* of our vision, the distortions from accuracy, deviations from the straight line. Photographic precision is only an accepted version of deformation. Error establishes itself as one persistent principle of Proust's universe, error in both social and the subjective domains. Within this skewed world Marcel erects and clings to three structures that offer temporary habitation to the questing mind. There is the refuge of habit, which allows us to adjust to new surroundings and people by becoming blind to all but the parts we can put to our own personal use; the refuge of laws, which define and explain the mystery of human behavior without penetrating it; and the refuge of the comic, which perceives the ridiculousness of both the above procedures and enjoys it without surpassing it.

Marcel's comedy of errors continues until he and
we begin to understand that art itself is an optic,
but a superior optic which will finally transform
error into truth for our mortal eyes. ". . . The
original painter or the original writer proceeds like
an oculist. The treatment he prescribes—by his
painting or his writing—is not always agreeable.
When he has finished, he tells us: 'Now have a
look.' And all at once the world, which was not
created only once, but it is created as often as a
new artist comes along, appears to us perfectly clear
—so different from the former world" (Preface to
P. Morand, *Tendres Stocks*; cf. II 1155). "The as-
semblage of rational processes we call vision" can be
restored to its purity through "the optical illusion"
of art (II 419/I 1018). The concentration of incidents and figures illustrating that the solitude and
suffering of art will lead to a new vision occurs in
the last two hundred pages, a section which had
been written in large part at the same time as the
opening volume. Not only are all the principal "or-
ders"—social, individual, and subjective—of Proust's
novel continually cast in optical terms, the ultimate
transformation of all experience by art also finds
expression in figures of vision and illusion.

At this point it would be utterly inadequate to
abandon this analysis with a statement to the effect
that in Proust it is the sense of sight that dominates.
For all human beings except the blind, the primacy
of sight among our faculties has been accompanied
by an extreme refinement of the eye and high development of the brain areas linked to that organ.

Unless one has something more particular than this in mind in speaking of Proust, it is equally meaningful to speak of the hypersensitivity of his olfactory sense or of his hearing. It is exactly my purpose, however, to bring out a specific quality of Proust's vision, a quality that is implicit in his imagery, that helps reveal the final significances of his art, and that has till now gone practically without notice. Why did Proust regularly turn to optics for his images? Are they appropriate to the total structure of his work? To what degree do these figures convey a meaning that he could not express otherwise? The answers will carry us far into Proust's universe.[3]

II

In the lengthy passage quoted earlier, the device
that repeatedly underscores the optical aspect of
the several mental distortions is the simple word,
"image." It is too often overlooked that in Proust
the basic unit of subjective life, despite its perpetual
flow, is something fixed and describable even if distorted: the image. Like Locke and Condillac (and
later Sartre), Proust saw our image-making faculty
as a means both for grasping the world and for
detaching ourselves from it, the essentially double
process of consciousness. Inevitably "image" spawns
a large family of photographic terms: *photographie*,
épreuve (proof), *cliché* (negative), *instantané* (still
or snapshot). And I have given them in an order
of increasing preciseness and appropriateness to
Proust's application, an order which he seems to
have sensed. For *instantané*, the arrested instant

of time, became one of his favorite words in *Le Temps retrouvé*. To this cluster of easily recognizable terms we must add the innocent-looking word *pan* (section, side, spot). What the magic lantern cast on the wall at Combray was a *pan* of Geneviève de Brabant's chateau (1 9/1 8); at the start, all that remains of Combray in Marcel's memory is a *pan lumineux* (1 43/1 33) showing a fragmentary view of the house and life within it; what exalts and distresses Bergotte at the moment of his death in the art gallery is a *petit pan de mur* painted by Vermeer (III 187/II 509), symbol of every effect he was himself unable to capture in writing. In all three cases this tiny neutral syllable carries more force than a specific photographic term. Its vagueness emphasizes the sense of a visual fragment that has lost all relation to reality except the capacity to suggest something lost, something infinitely worth seeking. Optics furnishes a vocabulary that implies fixed units of observation and retention. When the testimony of our senses reaches the mind, it becomes image. But—and here's both the rub and the way out—never one only: *many images*, in rapid and delayed and intermittent succession, and for the most part contradictory.

Néanmoins, au moment de ma découverte, la nature de M. Verdurin me présenta une face nouvelle insoupçonnée; et je conclus à la difficulté de présenter une image fixe aussi bien d'un caractère que des sociétés et des passions. Car il ne change pas moins qu'elles, et si on

veut clicher ce qu'il a de relativement immua-
ble, on le voit présenter successivement des
aspects différents (impliquant qu'il ne sait pas
garder l'immobilité, mais bouge) à l'objectif
déconcerté. (III 327)

Nevertheless, at the moment of my discovery,
M. Verdurin's character offered me a new and
unsuspected aspect; and I had to concede the
difficulty of presenting a fixed image of a character as much as of societies and of passions.
For character changes as much as they do, and
if one wishes to photograph [clicher] its rela-
tively immutable aspect, one can only watch
as it presents in succession different appearances (implying it does not know how to keep
still, but keeps moving) to the disconcerted
lens. (II 608, translation revised)

Though it remains the basic unit of observation
and memory, the single *instantané* turns out to be
an orphan, a meaningless fragment snatched out
of the flux. The still camera must yield to other
optical devices to provide metaphors for our pursuit of reality: the magic lantern, the kaleidoscope,
the cinematograph. All three depend upon a succession of images and describe the flux by reproducing it in a schematic form. They reflect time by
partially submitting to its ceaseless modifications.

A succession of contradictory images going under one name and "passing" by convention as a
single person or sentiment or social entity—this is
probably the most striking aspect of Proust's universe

to the unprepared reader. In this respect he reveals himself a creature of his age, a fact which by no means strips him of originality in his literary work. His vision was not of a unified, comprehensible, and essentially motionless world like that of Renaissance art, Albertian perspective, and the psychology of types and temperaments. The character Saint-Loup, for example, first appears as an insolent, unapproachable, exceedingly chic young aristocrat who will not deign to look at Marcel, and then within two pages he turns out to be the most loyal and considerate of friends. One paragraph later, he reveals himself as not merely a republican suspicious of the aristocratic principles he first seemed to incarnate, but a socialist who has steeped himself in Nietzsche and Proudhon. Three hundred pages later we watch him in the role of the headstrong, jealous lover of the actress Rachel, and blind to the extravagance of his own behavior. In his next transformation, after an equal interval, he has become simultaneously a selfish and cruel husband and a philandering homosexual keeping mistresses in order to cover up his carryings-on with young men. And yet Saint-Loup turns out in the end to be the major character in the novel who is killed in combat, a patriot and a true hero.

A similar series of mutations is followed in practically every development of character and action. The stations of Swann's love for Odette begin and end in indifference, and between those terms his sentiments, still covered by the generic word "love," pass through well-defined stages: esthetic appreciation of Odette's beauty, passive acceptance of her company, suffering because of being deprived of her company, urgent physical need for her, brief happiness in the satisfaction of that need, the torments of jealousy, social disgrace in her eyes because of his importunate behavior, a sense of physical and nervous sickness, despair at the recollection of his happier moments, incapacity to act in order to rescue himself, and the slow cooling of affection. Only afterwards, when the subjective emotions of love have been exhausted, does he marry Odette, an insignificant event which takes place off stage, barely mentioned. Not one image, but a mulitude. The action of the first twenty-eight hundred pages out of three thousand can be seen as consisting in Marcel's gradual discovery and acceptance of the truth that no person, no action, no sentiment, no social phenomenon is ever simple or consistent. Most of the way through, *A la recherche* remains a book of disenchantments. Things are never what they seem.

During these sections of the work, however, the heterogeneity of images, of *instantanés*, occasionally seems to graze a sense of order, to come into phase with itself. Odette turns out to be (or have been?) the "lady in pink" with whom Marcel's uncle consorted, as well as Elstir's mistress and his model in the costume of Miss Sacripant. Elstir turns out to be the "Biche" of Madame Verdurin's salon. Saint-Loup's mistress, Rachel, turns out to be the same "Rachel quand du seigneur" whose charms Marcel declined as a youth in a *maison de passe* with Bloch. These identifications suggest to Marcel some form of truth he does not yet understand. On the other hand, two of his most grievous moments occur when an expected identification is not made: first when he fails to recognize his grandmother the day he comes upon her suddenly and sees her as an old lady, and second when on her death bed she fails to recognize him. (At the very last she appears to respond to his kiss, but her actions are ambiguous.) Meanwhile Marcel has lived through a whole series of misapprehensions, which occur when he tries to verify the present against past experience or expectation. Every name which has enthralled him loses its magic. Similarly his ideals. Love, the elect world of nobility, memory, even the prestige of art and the sense of one's own identity disintegrate into a set of fragmentary experiences. Marcel is reduced to living with a collection of meaningless "stills," and it is exactly thus that he describes himself at the end of the passage on page 15. His failure to recognize himself is as ludicrous as the puzzlement one feels before a mislabeled painting.

But the second half of the last volume, *Le Temps retrouvé*, brings a total reversal of the action. Following Marcel's prolonged absence from Paris and from the places and people he has frequented, he returns. As he crosses Paris in a carriage, he undergoes an interior shift in sensibility, an ascension (expressed in an airplane image) above both past and present. Nevertheless he arrives in complete discouragement in front of the Prince de Guermantes' house, when suddenly, and fortuitously it seems, he experiences, five times in close succession,

what he has ceased to know since the very early stages
of the book: a *moment bienheureux,* a moment of
pleasure and communion caused by an involuntary
memory. He recognizes the past inhabiting the
present. Immediately thereafter, when he enters
the salon of the Prince de Guermantes, he undergoes, ten times in close succession, a complementary
but different experience. He comes upon ten as-
sorted figures out of his past, all of whom he fails at
first to recognize because of their "disguise" and
travestied appearance. Yet he finally contrives to
"give a name to the faces" (III 926/II 1034). The
entire final sequence is foreshadowed by the invitation to attend this *matinée chez le prince de Guermantes.* For after looking at the invitation, Marcel
discovers that the name "Guermantes" has resumed
its initial condition of "a name I did not recognize"
(III 857/II 984).

The remaining two hundred pages of the novel
form the heart of the labyrinth and conceal the only
egress from it. In a gigantic confrontation scene
Marcel finally re-identifies the elements of the world
that formerly had crystallized around that name of
Guermantes. The essential point about these last
pages, however, is not the fact that he stumbles
back over his past and finds it, but the fact that in
coming upon it again, his own subjective processes
have to follow a new order of events. In the past,
Marcel has experienced a series of encounters with
particularly alluring strangers who, after a number
of wild surmises in Marcel's mind about their character and station, are finally identified by name as

individuals of particular prestige and eminence in Marcel's universe. In this way he meets or sees at a distance Gilberte at Tansonville (1 140 ff./1 108 ff.), Mme. de Guermantes in the church at Combray (1 174 ff./1 134 ff.), Berma in the theater (1 448/1 344), Charlus at Balbec (1 751 ff./1 568 ff.), and Elstir at Rivebelle (1 825/1 621-22). In each case the incident terminates in an identification by name. (The first appearances of Bergotte and Saint-Loup entail slight variations.)

At the end of the novel, however, in the reversed order of events, Marcel begins with a familiar name and confronts at approximately the same time an individual "changed beyond recognition," to go with that name. Out of this dilemma he finally wins through to recognition. Each of the first ten cases following fast on Marcel's entry into the Prince's *matinée* (III 920-52/II 1031-1054) observes this order with minor variations and irregularities. At the fourth repetition, the nature of this little "act" has become perfectly clear to Marcel, and he states how much he must rely upon the cuing contained in a name.

Pourtant, comme j'aurais fait de l'idée de souveraineté ou de vice, qui ne tarde pas à donner un visage nouveau à l'inconnu, avec qui on aurait fait si aisément, quand on avait encore les yeux bandés, la gaffe d'être insolent ou aimable, et dans les mêmes traits de qui on discerne maintenant quelque chose de distingué ou de suspect, je m'appliquais à introduire dans le visage de l'inconnue, entièrement inconnue, l'idée qu'elle était Mme. Sazerat, et je finissais par rétablir le sens autrefois connu de ce visage, mais qui serait resté vraiment aliéné pour moi, entièrement celui d'une autre personne ayant autant perdu tous les attributs humains que j'avais connus, qu'un homme redevenu singe, si le nom et l'affirmation de l'identité ne m'avaient mis, malgré ce que le problème avait d'ardu, sur la voie de la solution. (III 931)

However, just as I would have done in the case of the stranger if I had started out with the assumption of royalty (or vice) which very quickly detects in his features something distinguished (or suspicious)—whereas, with one's eyes bandaged, it would have been so easy to commit the blunder of being disrespectful (or friendly)—I made a determined effort to apply to the face of an entirely unknown woman the idea that she was Mme. Sazerat, and ultimately I reconstituted the old familiar significance of her face, which would have remained utterly strange to me, wholly that of another woman who had lost all the human attributes familiar to me as fully as would a man who turned into a monkey, if her name and the assertion of her identity had not put me on the track of the solution, notwithstanding the difficult nature of the problem. (II 1039)

The ageless unchanging Odette provides a comic variation on the established pattern of name, nonrecognition, recognition. Marcel comes upon her tenth among his encounters with the past, when his mind has begun to adjust itself to the visible passage of time in people's physical appearance. "In her case, if I didn't recognize her at first, it was not because she had but because she hadn't changed" (III 948/II 1051). By this time a fundamental shift has taken place in the nature of a name, a sound which for the young Marcel could create the magic and prestige of unknown creatures. No longer a summation of mysteries, the name here acts only as a convenience or reminder, a means to a different end. Clearly that end is recognition, a final reconciliation and acceptance of conflicting images, not by any logical process but rather by an enlarged vision developed in the long experience of life itself. The tiny defiant convention of a name kept over the years challenges this mature vision to find a unity in multiplicity.

In recognition, we must ourselves now recognize the basic mental act of the entire novel, Marcel's ultimate achievement. Proust has, of course, treated this theme in earlier texts. Its first systematic expression comes in *Jean Santeuil* (II 222-34) when, after a chapter on the difficulties and rewards of recognizing places we have known, Proust describes how Jean "rediscovered impressions" of the ocean at Begmeil and analyzes his "esthetic pleasure." Swann's pleasure and pain in listening to *la petite phrase de Vinteuil* arises from the fact that he both succeeds and fails to recognize in those notes a part of himself to which he has no other access. He almost, *but not quite*, re-experiences the whole intermittent history of his love and jealousy (1 208ff./1 159ff., 304/234, 345ff./264ff., 529ff./404ff.). The seascape at Begmeil led Jean only to a vague "sensation of a permanent life," and Vinteuil's music evoked for Swann only the "apparition" of a woman. The ultimate meaning of A *la recherche du temps perdu* lies beyond either of these moments, and in trying to grasp it I shall have to give a sharp wrench to the generally accepted interpretation of Proust's esthetics.

The dozen or so unevenly distributed *moments bienheureux* produced by involuntary memory contain what first appears to be the essence of Proust-Marcel's profoundest sense of reality—a fleeting re-creation of the past in the present, conferring a rare and pleasurable sensation of timelessness. The sense of literary vocation seems to arise out of the desire to capture and fix this experience. The case is clearest in the *clochers de Martinville* passage where the adolescent Marcel notes down his impressions on the spot. But any literary outcome is obstructed in the sudden and overwhelming sequence of *moments bienheureux* near the end, just before Marcel enters the Prince's salon (III 865-88/ II 991-1007). In this latter passage he makes two references to the work before him: once to speak of its "great difficulties" (III 870-71/II 995), and later, in a lengthy meditation on how to "fix" the "image" of these instants, to ask himself: "Now, this means, which seemed to me the only one, what was it other than to create a work of art?" (III 879/II 1001). The sadness and reluctance of Proust-Marcel's tone here, the very deviousness of the syntax in the question, suggest that the sequence may not be complete after all. We feel the need of some further development in the action to carry us beyond these irresolute statements. The following thirty pages (III 888-918/II 1007-1029) of discursive writing on literature do not contain any new incidents and were probably intercalated late in the composition of the manuscript. Only when Marcel enters the Prince's salon does the action move again, in just the series of recognitions I have been belaboring. People, not objects or landscapes or sensations, fill these pages. In addition to the new order of events which devalues the magic of name in favor of a literal double take (an apt coinage which describes an action in two beats resembling a twin snapshot) these concluding pages establish a rising tension between Marcel's present circumstances and his literary vocation.

It begins with a clear challenge to his resolve.

En effet, dès que j'entrai dans le grand salon, bien que je tinsse toujours ferme en moi, au point où j'en étais, le projet que je venais de former, un coup de théâtre se produisit qui allait élever contre mon entreprise la plus grave des objections . . . Au premier moment je ne compris pas pourquoi j'hésitais à reconnaître le maître de maison, les invités, et pourquoi

chacun semblait s'être "fait une tête," gé-
néralement poudrée et qui les changeait com-
plètement. (III 920)

What happened was that, the moment I entered the drawing room, although I was hold-
ing firmly in mind the project I had just formed
as far as I had worked it out, a *coup de théâtre*
occurred which was destined to raise the gravest
of objections against my undertaking . . . The
first instant, I did not understand why I could
not immediately recognise the master of the
house and the guests, who seemed to have
"made themselves up," usually with powdered
hair, in a way that completely changed their
appearance. (II 1031)

The effect of the next one hundred and twenty
pages slowly forms as one of powerful literary suspense. Can Marcel's project survive in the face of
the enormous effort required of him to recognize
the very creatures about whom he proposes to write
his novel? It is a crucial test. As the ten odd figures
loom up before him, he doubts once again every
resolution he made a few moments earlier after the
spasm of *moments bienheureux*. Yet a new realiza-
tion comes to him gradually, a revelation which
could not be made by the objects and sensations
associated with the *moments bienheureux*, but only
by people. It is the reality and meaning of death.

En effet, "reconnaître" quelqu'un, et plus encore, après n'avoir pas pu le reconnaître, l'iden-

tifier, c'est penser sous une seule dénomination
deux choses contradictoires, c'est admettre que
ce qui était ici, l'être qu'on se rappelle n'est
plus, et que ce qui y est, c'est un être qu'on ne
connaissait pas; c'est avoir à penser un mystère
presque aussi troublant que celui de la mort
dont il est, du reste, comme la préface et
l'annonciateur. (III 939)

And in truth, to "recognise" someone and, more
especially, to work out his identity after not
having been able to recognise him, means con-
ceiving two contradictory things under the
same denomination; it means admitting that
what used to be here, the person we remember,
no longer exists, while the one that is here we
did not know; it means having to penetrate a
mystery almost as disturbing as death, of which
it is, as it were, the preface and the forerunner.
(II 1044)

The complex shuffling and sorting out of images
which we call "recognizing" a person contains the
idea of death, and the idea of death spurs Marcel
on anew toward his "urgent, capital rendezvous
with himself" (III 986/II 1079). And Marcel is in
effect going through the same set of reactions to
himself as to everyone else he encounters. After the
superficial assertion of his new vocation during the
moments bienheureux, he fails to recognize himself
in that role any longer when he enters the salon. His
masquerade as writer is no more convincing than
anyone else's. At least so it seems at the start.

Meanwhile his sense of vocation has had two more rude setbacks, which prolong the suspense. Not having been given the essential clue of a name, he totally fails to recognize his childhood sweetheart, Gilberte, and afterwards, the actress Rachel. He feels as if he had failed an examination (III 980/ ———). The *matinée* moves towards its climax—or rather the climax of Marcel's life approaches in the grotesque zoological setting of elegant society. And we are carefully prepared for it. Gilberte goes to find her daughter, Mlle. de Saint-Loup, to introduce her to Marcel. Four pages are devoted to establishing in her absence how she embodies the entire action of the book in its orientation between the *deux côtés*. And when at last Marcel turns his attention to the approaching girl of sixteen, he sees more than he has seen in any other person in his life. Since he has never met her before, he cannot recognize her—or rather, he can recognize only those aspects which reveal her relation to what he does know. Thus he recognizes in her "my Youth." In the very next sentence the innocent pronoun *elle* gently associates Mlle. de Saint-Loup with his thoughts on time, and he recognizes her as far more.

Enfin cette idée du Temps avait un dernier prix pour moi, elle était un aiguillon, elle me disait qu'il était temps de commencer si je voulais atteindre ce que j'avais quelquefois senti au cours de ma vie, dans de brefs éclairs, du côté de Guermantes, dans mes promenades en voiture avec Mme. de Villeparisis, et qui m'avait

fait considérer la vie comme digne d'être vécue.
(III 1032)

And lastly, this idea of time had a final value
for me; it was like a goad, reminding me that
it was time to begin if I wished to achieve
what I had occasionally in the course of my life
sensed in brief flashes, along the Guermantes
way or while driving with Mme. de Villeparisis,
and which had encouraged me to regard life as
worth living. (II 1112)

She incarnates a new idea of time, not death only,
but youth. Her beauty as of a "masterpiece" is the
spur to Marcel to begin his work. She *is* his vocation, not merely its symbol, but the work of art in
the flesh, which he must have the courage to reproduce in its lengthy gestation and its final fullness.

This is the last incident in the book. Marcel
simply vanishes without stage stuff from the Prince's
salon and meditates for fifteen pages upon the
urgency and magnitude of his work. There is no
longer the slightest uncertainty about his application to that work except for the possible interruption of death. Marcel has found his youth, not in
the past but in the present.

I have taken a long time in this rehearsal of the
end of A *la recherche* for what I consider important
reasons. The much touted *moments bienheureux* do
not bring Marcel to his vocation or confer on him
any lasting happiness. They represent an important
step toward both those ends, or more accurately,

they are the guideposts which show him the right
direction without themselves taking him to his
goal except by anticipation. The multiple sequence
they contribute toward the end functions as a
preliminary to the *dénouement* of the book, not
as its true climax. The attitude of passivity on
which they rely and the tendency they have to en-
courage the substitution of pleasure for effort, and
objects for people, prevent them from offering the
key to Marcel's salvation. In this exact sense, most
of Proust's commentators have gone astray. *The
ultimate moment of the book is not a* moment
bienheureux *but a recognition.* Coming after a prolonged sequence of preparatory and parallel re-
identifications, the final step brings Marcel to a true
self-recognition.

It is revealing to imagine the different ways in
which this end might have been accomplished. For
instance, Proust could have turned the tables on
Marcel and let him squirm while an old acquaint-
ance fails to hide the difficulty he has in recognizing
the narrator. This variant of the hunter hunted or
the mocker mocked would have forced Marcel to
acknowledge the whole apparatus of naming, nonrecognition, death of former selves, and identification as directed at himself. Or, in another equally
comic version, Proust might have let Marcel glimpse
a disturbingly familiar figure across the room—so
familiar and so impossible of recognition that he
retraces his steps to try to establish the identity of
this *instantané.* And after a fruitless scrutiny of the
assembled ancients, Marcel would suddenly discern

his prey—a clouded reflection of himself in a mirror half hidden behind the guests. Still, there is something a little inept and contrived about both these possible incidents. At the end of a novel unflaggingly subjective in orientation, Proust chose to exteriorize this ultimate incident and expose its full meaning in the flesh. In a young girl he has never seen before, Marcel at last recognizes his past and his death, his youth and his hope: his vocation. What distinguished all these recognitions, and especially the last, from the *moments bienheureux* is that the recognitions contain an active participation of the mind, a conscious resolve to identify a person at first unknown. The perpetually elusive pleasure of the *moments bienheureux,* as in the *clochers de Martinville* scene, can occasionally lead to a provisional form of literary expression. But the joy and the vocation last a few moments only. After the supreme rite of recognition at the end, the provisional nature of life disappears in the discovery of the straight and narrow path of art.

When we come to the phrases about the *moments bienheureux* making "death indifferent" (III 867/II 992) and life mediocre, we may believe prematurely that Marcel has reached the last stage of the journey. But not so, for it turns out to be a transitory elevation of mind which will soon fail him. He has to go on to the experience that will make every moment of life not mediocre but crucially important and reveal death not as indifferent but as the event which defines life and is to be feared only because it sets a limit to one's human capacity to create (III 1038/II 1116). Proust-Marcel's transcendence comes back to earth at the end in unequivocal terms.

Were this not true, the structure of Proust's novel would be open to severe criticism. The role of the *moments bienheureux* in the action ceases two hundred pages before the end, and had the novel stopped there, a perfect circle could be drawn through this final scene and the early experience of the *madeleine*. And it would be a vicious circle of fascination with a fleeting passive pleasure in fortuitous recollection, and of hesitation over a literary calling almost but not quite embraced. The triumph of Marcel's career and Proust's novel lies in the fact that the circle is broken just in time and a larger, more responsible, more mature act asserts itself in the form of recognition. When completely realized as self-recognition, it leads Marcel not into reverie but into the work of art. The effort required, the direction voluntarily chosen, the renunciation of lesser pleasures and illusions to serve a larger end— all these aspects of self-recognition give it a moral significance which the *moments bienheureux* never achieve. They represent a primitive and elusive stage of what Marcel attains only at the end, and they are all he has to hold onto for many years— all we have to hold onto for three thousand pages. For the dedicated reader of Proust, the suspense is terrific, especially at the end.

III

In considering how Marcel finally discovered order in the succession of contradictory *instantanés* life offers us, I have overrun myself and gone right through to the conclusion of the novel. These distinctions between involuntary memory and conscious recognition appear to me absolutely basic to a proper understanding of the action of the novel as well as of its structure and its esthetic. But I have rushed right by one of the central questions: Why do these two related classes of experience bring with them a particular sense of reward—a sensuous *pleasure*, or an esthetic sense of beauty and reality in life? Marcel himself states that it was the sense of pleasure which alerted him to take particular notice of these moments (i 45/i 34, iii 867/ ii 992). To explain as some critics have that the reward attained flows out of a partial or complete act of creation merely displaces the question. What then is the reward of art? Moreover most of these privileged moments seem far removed from the dedication and discipline of art. As is never true in the case of his vast diversionary skirmishes with love and social ambition, Marcel has here found something to make life worth living. For full understanding we must seek far beyond the idle pleasures of reminiscence.

On leaving a dinner party of the Duchesse de Guermantes in a carriage Marcel reflects on the boring conversations he has just had at the party. Yet in looking back at them he experiences a fleeting "exaltation." The sentence which explains his state of mind is crucial. He is speaking of the fresh images in his mind of the evening's events. "I had just slid them into the interior stereoscope by means of which, as soon as we are no longer ourselves, as soon as, endowed with a worldly attitude, we wish to receive our life only from others, we give high relief to what they have said, to what they have done" (II 548/I 1107). At this early stage of his esthetic education, Marcel has deceived himself about the evening he has just spent and exaggerates its value. The metaphor of the stereoscope to represent the transformations of subjective process takes on meaning far beyond this context. It is increasingly in such optical terms that Proust gave figurative expression to his sense of art and reality. When Marcel cannot recognize the three trees near Balbec which seem to have particular significance, he wonders if it all could be due to "visual fatigue which made me see them double in time as one sometimes sees double in space" (I 719/I 545)—an optical illusion of memory. Later, in Balbec, he is attracted by the odor of hawthorn blooms: "I went nearer but my eyes did not know at what adjustment [*cran*] to set their optical mechanism in order to see the flowers at the same time along the hedge and in myself" (II 786n/——). In the closing volume, after a passage on art which concludes with a sentence on the "depth" of a work which "recomposes life," he speaks of the lesser truths of the intelligence. "As for the truths which the intelligence —even of the most exalted minds—gathers in open work, straight ahead, fully lit, their value may be very great; but they have dry flat outlines and no depth, because no depth had to be crossed in order to reach them, because they have not been recreated" (III 898/II 1015). A few pages later Proust adds: "And more than the painter, who has to have seen many churches to paint a single one, the writer, in order to obtain volume and consistency, generality and literary reality, needs many beings for a single sentiment" (III 907/II 1021). Depth, or what is called in optics penetration effect, cannot be found in a single image, a single *instantané*. The visible world reaches us through a double take based on the stereoscopic principle. Two slightly different versions of the same "object" from our two eyes are combined subjectively with the effect of relief. The binocular nature of human vision is achieved through some of the most delicate adjustments of which our organism is capable. Normally we confine this stereoscopic effect, which gives an impress of reality in depth to the world around us, to perception in space. Proust undertakes a transposition of spatial vision into a new faculty. The accumulation of optical figures in A la recherche gradually removes our depth perception from space and re-erects it in time. When we finally reach Le Temps retrouvé, the transplanting has been completed and there can be no doubt about the nature of recognition and involuntary memory. These two examples of response to our own past embody in different degrees the *optics of time*. Proust wrote out of an inner vision trained on time itself. As boldly as Minkowskian geometry his enormous novel revolutionizes our sense of "here" and "now."

The allusion to Minkowsky, who succeeded in graphing the space-time principle of Einstein's special relativity, has more than casual pertinence. Relativity tells us that no object *by itself* has either definable location or measurable velocity. Two objects are required to yield a relative reading, and there is no universal grid like the ether to give an absolute figure. An object can be described as located somewhere and in a certain motion only in reference to what is about it. And so it is also with memories or experiences. One alone would disappear under our scrutiny, like a star or a dial stared at too long. Physiologically and psychologically and metaphysically, *to see* means to see with or against or beside something. The school of Gestalt psychology has long since developed this simple truth of the relativity of perception: we grasp things juxtaposed in clusters, framed by one another. A good deal of irresponsible speculation has attempted to associate Proust with Einstein and the principle of relativity; in his letters to Vettard, Proust himself was party to it. But here we can see the particular respect in which Proust's treatment of memory, as always multiple, implies a relativity principle in consciousness itself based on an optics of time.[4]

As always, Proust makes every effort to declare his intentions; he has no interest in hiding his hand except to play his cards at the right moment. And even this he often does badly. One of his earliest texts, written at a time when he had a kind of fetish on eyes, describes a moment of reverie. "Then the most beautiful eyes in the world . . . are nothing more . . . than 'time machines,' telescopes of the invisible." (*Pastiches et mélanges*, 214) But the closing portion of *A la recherche* employs a carefully planned series of comparisons that re-align our visual and optical faculties in the direction of time. When memory fails Marcel, we are told: "There are optical errors in time as there are in space" (III 593/II 799). The insufficiency of Marcel's multiple *moments bienheureux* before entering the prince's salon, the incompleteness of his experience "of the essence of things," is described thus: "But this *trompe-l'œil* which brought close to me a moment of the past incompatible with the present, this *trompe-l'œil* did not last" (III 873/II 996). The faulty optics of the *moments bienheureux* has been rectified fifty pages later when he begins the feat of recognizing the cast of performers, of whom he is himself one. "Time . . . claims them in order to project its magic lantern on them. . . . Thus the new and so unrecognizable Argencourt was like a revelation of Time, which he had rendered partially visible" (III 924/II 1033). *Time* occurs now with a capital T, meaning as revealed by stereoscopy, in relief.

Par tous ces côtés, une matinée comme celle où je me trouvais était quelque chose de beaucoup plus précieux qu'une image du passé, mais m'offrait comme toutes les images successives, et que je n'avais jamais vues, qui séparaient le passé du présent, mieux encore, le rapport qu'il y avait entre le présent et le passé; elle était comme ce qu'on appelait autrefois une vue optique, mais une vue optique des années, la vue non d'un moment, non d'une personne située dans la perspective déformante du Temps. (III 925)

From all these aspects, an affair like the one I was attending was something far more precious than a picture of the past; it offered me, as it were, all the successive pictures separating the past from the present, which I had never seen, and, better yet, the relationship of the past to the present. It resembled what used to be called "an optical view," but of the years, the view not of a monument, not of a person placed in the distorting perspective of Time. (II 1034, translation revised)

The true optics of Time give us an accurate and lasting image in depth. The faulty version of the text in the original edition (which substitutes "but" for the last "not") seriously distorts the meaning. Moreover, the word "time" at the end would be more consistent in lower case, for it refers to the flux from which the multiple optical view removes us.

Proust restates all this visual imagery of time in his last letter (1922) to Camille Vettard, where he extends a figure already used in the closing pages of his novel (III 1041/II 118). His novel, he writes to Vettard, "has grown out of the application of a special sense . . . which is very difficult to describe. . . . The image (imperfect as it is) which seems to me best suited to convey the nature of that special sense is that of a telescope, a telescope pointed at time, for a telescope renders visible for us stars invisible to the naked eye, and I have tried to render visible to the consciousness unconscious phenomena, some of which, having been entirely forgotten, are situated in the past" (*Correspondance générale*, III 194).

Proust set about to make us *see time*. But the telescope figure is not so apt as that of the stereoscope. To see anything in temporal depth, we need at least two impressions of it. One image, one present, is not enough, because a single event or impression isolated in the consciousness cannot sustain itself, has no dimensionality in time, remains "flat" to the mind; it can be kept alive only by voluntary memory or the sheer uncreative repetition of habit. In the final reassembling of all the characters, Marcel recognizes them one by one—that is he succeeds in slipping side by side into his "interior stereoscope" the different images of, say, Odette. She is, *simultaneously*, cocotte and fashionable hostess, wife and widow, mother and grandmother, and newly acquired mistress of the senile Duc de Guermantes, who in the past refused to admit her to his wife's receptions. Memory, in its alternate form of recognition, progressively sets one image beside other chronologically separated images and sees in them not change (though this is the comical "masked ball" aspect of the final scene which precedes recognition), not *trompe l'œil*, but revelation of true identity, the "optical view." Odette is all that. At last Marcel knows who the characters are that he has encountered all his life, different each time, and classified by necessity and habit under names. Multiplicity now brings not confusion but dimensionality and depth. Memory in Proust's sense designates a stereoscopic or "stereologic" consciousness which sees the world simultaneously (and thus out of time) in relief. Merely to remember something is meaningless unless the remembered image is combined with a moment in the present affording a view of the same object or objects. Like our eyes, our memories must see double; those two images then converge in our minds into a single heightened reality.

With the provision that we imagine it employing several simultaneous images and not two only, the stereoscope comparison will carry us still further toward understanding Proust's treatment of time. A mere succession of images, unequally retained and seen without uniform clarity, produces an effect of "volume," as Marcel finds watching Albertine in her flickering moods (III 372-73/II 641). But a fuller grasp of the object comes only when all images, including the closest, have been brought to rest "on a uniform plane"—just as two stereopticon views must be equidistant from our eyes. The act of ultimate recognition removes all images from the stream of time to set them up temporally equidistant in Time, equally available to our consciousness. And then we are no longer pinned to the present looking backwards, we are no longer bathed helplessly in the Heraclitean flux or the Bergsonian *durée*. The act of involuntary memory, fleetingly, and the act of recognition more permanently, wrench themselves free of clock time to find a perspective vast enough to hold all our experience. In fact, the vivid but transitory nature of the *moments bienheureux* can probably be traced to the fact that they result from so violent a readjustment in time that chronology is inverted and the past appears closer than the present. Such is the oddly unreal but convincing perspective that supports Combray, rising like a flower out of a cup of tea; and such a point of view returns for a time with the *moments bienheureux* at the end. Fittingly enough a term to describe this inverted perspective can be found in the technical vocabulary of optics. Pseudoscopic effect means precisely reverse relief: near is far and far is near. Certain kinds of optical apparatus, like certain forms of writing, can produce this vivid distortion of reality. The opening of Proust's novel creates an alluring pseudoscopic effect in which the past both haunts and hypnotizes the present. But not so the close.[5]

Even though Proust made extensive and explicit use of optical imagery, he did not do so systematically or even with a full awareness of the importance these comparisons were going to take on. However, especially in *Le Temps retrouvé*, something approaching a table of value begins to take shape out of his terminology and repeated metaphors. It is for the most part the negative statements in the last volume, statements which attack a certain form of limited vision, that allow us to distinguish between three basic ways of seeing the world —or of recreating it. Each one develops a fundamental means of assembling the multiplicity of images or *instantanés* that make up our first impression of Proust's universe—and of life itself.

1. The *cinematographic principle* employs a sequence of separately insignificant differences to produce the effect of motion or animation in objects seen. It vividly conveys the sensation of flux, of a steady linear change from one moment flowing into the next. Thus a series of stills in sequence can create the illusion of movement when riffled through rapidly under our eyes or thrown on a screen. This is the simplest and most familiar of the three prin-

ciples, for it appears to conform to the continuity of normal experience.

2. The *montage principle* employs a succession of large contrasts to reproduce the disparity and contradiction that interrupt the continuity of experience. In the international vocabulary of film-making, montage is the term meaning the arrangement of shots or footage in an order designed to produce a particular effect. The most extreme theorist and practitioner of montage, Sergei Eisenstein, stated tersely that "Montage is conflict," and defined its particular property as consisting in "the fact that two film pieces of any kind, placed together, inevitably combine into a new concept, a new quality, arising out of that juxtaposition" ("Word and Image," in *The Film Sense*, p. 4). Montage can produce infinitely varied effects by mere arrangement. A serious intense face followed by a shot of a burial suggests grief; the same face followed by an opera performance suggests pleasurable concentration. The montage principle rejects the accumulation of small differences (cinematographic principle) for the exploitation of larger associative or dissociative leaps that suggest the meaning of a scene or situation by contrast. Its motion may be logical or whimsical, chronological or purely visual. Montage vividly conveys the sensation of intermittency or jump that remains in any grasp we have of life and the tendency of what we see and what we feel to resist any prolonged

order or linear sequence in time. The complex art form we call "the movies" employs both cinematographic and montage principles. The former without the latter would lead to monotony; the latter without the former would lead to incoherence.

3. The *stereoscopic principle* abandons the portrayal of motion in order to establish a form of arrest which resists time. It selects a few images or impressions sufficiently different from one another not to give the effect of continuous motion, and sufficiently related to be linked in a discernible pattern. This stereoscopic principle allows our binocular (or multiocular) vision of mind to hold contradictory aspects of things in the steady perspective of recognition, of relief in time.

Throughout the latter part of his work, Proust shuttled back and forth among these three versions of the world. Moreover, they occupy different positions in a hierarchy of value or truth. At the nadir of the entire action of the novel, when Marcel is about to enter Jupien's *maison de passe* during the war, he half recognizes as Saint-Loup a military figure that comes out. Marcel describes the man in purely cinematic terms, for he is struck by "the number of different points through which his body passed and the small number of seconds within which this exit, which resembled a sortie attempted by a besieged party, was executed" (III 810/II 951). The ambiguous identity is never resolved. However, a few pages later, when Marcel learns of Saint-Loup's death in combat, we encounter a far clearer version of things and a specific distinction between kinds of subjective vision.

Et l'avoir vu si peu en somme, en des sites si variés, dans des circonstances si diverses et sé-parées par tant d'intervalles . . . ne faisait que me donner de sa vie des tableaux plus frap-pants, plus nets, de sa mort un chagrin plus lucide, que l'on n'en a souvent pour des per-sonnes aimées davantage, mais fréquentées si continuellement que l'image que nous gardons d'elles n'est plus qu'une espèce de vague moy-enne entre une infinité d'images insensiblement différentes, et aussi que notre affection ras-sasiée n'a pas, comme pour ceux que nous n'avons vus que pendant des moments limités au cours de rencontres inachevées malgré eux et malgré nous, l'illusion de la possibilité d'une affection plus grande dont les circonstances seules nous auraient frustrés. (III 847)

And the very fact that I had after all seen him so seldom and in such varied settings, under such different circumstances and at such long intervals . . . only served to give me more clear-cut and striking pictures of his life and a more sharply defined sorrow over his death than we often have at the loss of someone we have loved more but with whom we have been so constantly associated that the mental picture we retain of him has become merely a sort of

hazy composite of an infinite number of pictures imperceptibly different—also, our affection having had full expression, we do not
nurse the illusion that we might have known a
richer relationship, had not circumstances
thwarted us, as we feel in the case of those
whom we have seen only for brief moments
and at meetings which were cut all too short,
through no fault of theirs or ours. (II 977-978)

The cinematographic memory of someone seen
so often as to yield many similar images is, therefore, inferior to the memory of someone seen in
widely separated and contrasting *tableaux*. Marcel's
memory of Saint-Loup hovers somewhere between
items two and three of my outline, and I am inclined to think that the separation of the two was
not entirely clear in Proust's mind. Nevertheless,
what he wrote about the nature of literature permits me to insist on their distinctness in his mind
from the successive cinematographic view.

Quelques-uns voulaient que le roman fût une
sorte de défilé cinématographique des choses.
Cette conception était absurde. Rien ne s'éloigne plus de ce que nous avons perçu en réalité
qu'une telle vue cinématographique. (III 882-
83)

Some wished the novel to be a sort of cinematographic parade. This conception was ab-
surd. In reality, nothing is farther removed
than this cinematographic view from what we
have perceived. (II 1003-1004)

Proust makes his clearest statement of the stereoscopic principle in an earlier volume, once again apropos of Saint-Loup.

Les êtres ne cessent pas de changer de place par rapport à nous. Dans la marche insensible mais éternelle du monde, nous les considérons comme immobiles, dans un instant de vision trop court pour que le mouvement qui les entraîne soit perçu. Mais nous n'avons qu'à choisir dans notre mémoire deux images prises d'eux à des moments différents, assez rapprochés cependant pour qu'ils n'aient pas changé en eux-mêmes, du moins sensiblement, et la différence des deux images mesure le déplacement qu'ils ont opéré par rapport à nous. (II 1021)

Other people never cease to change places in relation to ourselves. In the imperceptible but eternal march of the world, we regard them as motionless in a moment of vision, too short for us to perceive the motion that is sweeping them on. But we have only to select in our memory two pictures taken of them at different moments, close enough together however for them not to have altered in themselves— perceptibly, that is to say—and the difference between the two pictures is a measure of the displacement that they have undergone in relation to us. (II 299)

Now, it is terribly important to understand just what Proust is getting at in these long meditations

on how we behold the world. In rejecting the cinematographic or continuous vision of habit, he is
referring not only to categories of experience such
as I have set up, but also to artistic principles on
which he staked his entire novel and literary career.
Vision, optics seen large, is the link; ". . . for style
to a writer, just like color to a painter, is a question
not of technique but of vision" (III 895/II 1013).
"Style" must here be read in the broadest sense
both of structure and actual writing. We have now
reached the turn in the road from which we can
suddenly see how vision as style permitted Proust to
transcend successive time and create a work of
simultaneous time.

Ce que nous appelons la réalité est un certain
rapport entre ces sensations et ces souvenirs qui
nous entourent simultanément—rapport que
supprime une simple vision cinématographique,
laquelle s'éloigne par là d'autant plus du vrai
qu'elle prétend se borner à lui—rapport unique
que l'écrivain doit retrouver pour en enchaîner
à jamais dans sa phrase les deux termes différents. . . . Mais il y avait plus. Si la réalité
était cette espèce de déchet de l'expérience, à
peu près identique pour chacun, parce que
quand nous disons: un mauvais temps, une
guerre, une station de voitures, un restaurant
éclairé, un jardin en fleurs, tout le monde sait
ce que nous voulons dire; si la réalité était cela,
sans doute une sorte de film cinématographique
de ces choses suffirait et le "style", la "littéra-

ture" qui s'écarteraient de leur simples données seraient un hors-d'œuvre artificiel. (III 889-90)

What we call reality is a certain relationship between these sensations and the memories which surround us at the same time (a relationship that is destroyed by a bare cinematographic presentation, which gets further away from the truth the more closely it claims to adhere to it) the only true relationship, which the writer must recapture so that he may forever link together in his phrase its two distinct elements. . . . But there was more than that, I reflected. If reality were merely that by-product of existence, so to speak, approximately identical for everybody—because, when we say "bad weather, war, cab-stand, brightly lighted restaurant, garden in bloom," everybody knows what we mean—if reality were that, then naturally a sort of cinematographic film of these things would be enough and the "style" or the "literature" that departed from their simple theme would be an artificial *hors-d'œuvre*. (II 1008-1009)

Here in the margin we should write, as Proust did on occasion: *capital, à creuser*. No, art is not a side dish; reality is not a common "husk of experience." At last we come within reach of something that will hold our experience of the world together. The "relation between simultaneous sensations" encompasses the mental processes described as recognition and the stereoscopic principle. And in another sentence in this same passage (quoted in full on page 5) this relation is explicitly identified as "metaphor." In the subterranean region we have reached, the different aspects of art and reality communicate through large channels of correspondence. Metaphor, style, recognition, simultaneous sensation, stereoscopic vision—these terms describe both the weave of a novel and the texture of experience. The deep-flowing relationship between these two realms sustains the unity of Proust's vast domain and allows him to speak in the remainder of the passage quoted about writing as "translation" rather than invention in the ordinary sense.

By going back now for a moment to the three principles of vision or style, we can examine more closely the sense of Proust's phrase, "a certain relation between sensations," and even of "metaphor." Such expressions cannot be allowed to slip by as mere commonplaces, for they carry the burden of his meaning here.

Montage principle, the middle term of the three, does not come so explicitly as the other two under Proust's scrutiny, but his narrative cries out for this order of three attitudes, three styles. Our first experience of reality is cinematographic and linear, a primitive continuity that conveys a sense of cause and effect, of what is possible and what inevitable. Subsequently this secure sense of predictability is disrupted when we encounter contradictions and alterations in Nature and, above all, in people. This second phase of disenchantments, corresponding to the montage principle, makes one aware of conflict and contrast. Still later, unless we allow disillusionment and habit to extinguish completely our sense of irregularity and inscrutability in the world, a moment may occur in which our multifarious experience achieves an unexpected consistency with itself. Out of disorder a tentative pattern begins to appear. Without repeating themselves, certain events and sensations, usually the most trivial in appearance, recur in modified form and reinforce one another in a kind of overlay. *Similarity with a difference* means metaphor (not pure identity) and stereoscopic vision. It should now be fairly evident that these three stages of experience loosely correspond to periods of life we designate as youth (not childhood, whose vision is still unformed and free), maturity, and age—a pattern of enchantment, disenchantment, and re-enchantment. Few men succeed in carrying their lives fully into the third stage, which is the opposite of self-indulgent reminiscence.

This reference to the ages of man would be no more than a commonplace were it not for the fact that those simple steps clarify the divisions of Proust's novel and its most fundamental structure. Apart from the frame in which it is set and which anticipates the end of the novel, Combray describes in a comparatively simple narrative texture the enchantment of a young boy by the mysteries of the world. The advance of time alone, he believes, will lead him to understanding and happiness. But after the long parallel history of Swann, the shift of scene

to Balbec and Paris confronts Marcel with a series
of inexplicable and dismayingly inconsistent events.
The entire body of the novel—twenty-five hundred
pages of it—methodically overthrows the vision of
life Marcel enjoyed in Combray; only his mother
and grandmother (to whom he lives in such a close
relation that he sees them by cinematographic time)
survive the universal disaster. Even his artistic am-
bitions fade. Not until the end, after an interval
of absence from this semi-demented world of montage vision, does Marcel recover a sense of reality
by discovering in recognition the third station of
experience. And now we can place the *moments
bienheureux* within this progression somewhere between montage vision and stereoscopic vision. They
bring urgent yet fleeting signs of a true perspective
on life. This perspective, first suggested in the opening pages, slowly extinguishes itself through the
broad wastes of love and social climbing, and then
reappears transfigured at the end.

The most puzzling and the most crucial point
in this evolution comes exactly between the second
and third stages in the action of the novel. Up to
now I have systematically ignored this key question:
What carries Marcel from the fascinating but exasperating zigzags of montage (concentrated in the
wayward, iridescent person of Albertine) to the
final elevated vision? Is this not perhaps the weak
point in Proust's construction? Does he even bother
to make the transition? In bulk of words he passes
it over in relative silence: two laconic pages (III 854-
56/II 983-84). Does he not leave us in the dark on

the most momentous change in the whole work? To answer these questions, I shall pick up once more the train of thought, obsessive as it may be, that has propelled me this far. For the meanings of Proust's optical imagery are not yet exhausted, and in particular the controlling metaphor of a stereoscope which looks into time.

I have pointed out that the equidistance from the eyes of stereoptican views can suggest a total readjustment of present and past into equidistance in stereologic time. Thus we can establish a point of vantage outside of cinematographic and montage time. A second factor governing stereoscopic optics now reveals its pertinency to Proust's composition.

To perceive depth properly, our eyes are set apart in our heads by a distance that is proportionate to our size and our need to judge the distance of objects around us. Two eyes, separated by several yards would not serve us effectively, for our minds would not be able to assimilate and unify views of the world so divergent. The condition would produce an extreme effect. The interval between our human eyes permits us to register depths in space on our scale and instantaneously. In comparable fashion the interval between our mental eyepieces in time, the interval between juxtaposed impressions, must also be in scale to human life if they are to assume temporal depth. Now the chronology of *A la recherche* entails numerous complexities and has called forth a good many erroneous generalizations.[6] After forty-odd opening pages, which carefully avoid any relapse into calendar or clock time and take place in a kind of temporal limbo, the subsequent portions of the novel observe a reasonably clear chronological sequence. Temporal gaps are specified and allusions are made to future developments with a feeling of temporal and logical continuity. But as early as the middle of *Les Jeunes Filles en fleurs*, we run across this parenthesis, like a clue to the wary: "(our life being to so small a degree chronological, and interjecting so many anachronisms into the sequence of days)" (I 642/ I 488). As we advance into the central and latter portions of the novel, the chronology of the action, like the ages of the characters, becomes increasingly undefined and ambiguous—in part the result of Proust's perpetual inflation of the original text, but also the result of a sense of structure which carries all that bulk. Not until the opening pages of *Le Temps retrouvé* is the chronology finally specified again—by Marcel's three sojourns for "long years" in two *maisons de santé* and the advent of war in 1914 (III 723/II 893, 751/909, 755/912, 854/983). And appropriately it is here that a marginal comment on change of personality in several characters comes to a different conclusion from what we have been told earlier. "Everything is a matter of chronology" (III 737n/——). But the word means something far different now after the distance covered by the narrative, and at the crucial moment of change in perspective at the end, the chronology at stake is a temporal interval rather than a linear progression.

"The new *maison de santé* to which I returned

did not cure me any more than the first, and many years passed before I left it. During the train trip I made to return at last to Paris . . ." (III 854/ II 983). With so gentle and imperceptible a movement as this the tide begins to turn. One sentence of transition and, hidden away in it, two words we could easily miss: "many years." But Marcel's career and the approaching resolution of the novel depend on that barely stated temporal span; it corresponds to the spatial gap between our eyes. In order to perceive relief in time, our consciousness must behold, simultaneously, impressions removed from one another by "many years." And then Proust goes on to define that interval with increasing exactness as the duration of a complete social cycle. In referring to the unpredictable reception given writers by critics and the public, he states, "Their logomachy renews itself every ten years" (III 893/II 1012). Social change itself follows this pattern of self-renewal. "Moreover, it must be said that this ignorance of true situations, an ignorance which pushes to the top those who appear to be the elect in their present position, as if the past did not exist . . . is also an effect . . . of Time" (III 964/ II 1064). Newcomers to society benefit from this short memory, although for them the interval becomes slightly enlarged. "Now with strangers of this kind, thirty years later one recalls nothing precise which can project into the past and change the value of the being whom one has under one's eyes" (III 965/II 1064). And finally, in settling on a median figure, Proust identifies the interval of significant social change with the interval of significant individual change. In both cases a cycle is completed. "For if, in these twenty-year periods, the conglomerates of little coteries fall apart and reform according to the attraction of new stars, themselves destined moreover to move away and return, then also there takes place in the souls of being crystallizations and then crumblings followed by new crystallizations" (III 992/——). Twenty years, one now realizes, is the inner span of Proust's novel —not from one end to the other but from the middle of the period described in detail during the opening six volumes (approximately 1900) to the last sequence (approximately 1920). The wider range of ten to thirty years embraces all other portions of action pertaining to Marcel.

This does not mean that if we merely look back twenty years, we shall automatically have a new perspective on everything, a new vision or reality. If an image or sensation out of the past is to be truly recognized in the Proustian sense and not merely recollected, it must be summoned back by a related experience in the present and after a period of absence. For, if an image remains constantly present, it obeys the cinematographic principle, freezes into habit, and can be manipulated only by the intelligence. The original experience or image must have been forgotten, completely forgotten, a circumstance which turns the elapsed years into a true gap. This is Proust's "general law of memory." True memory or recognition surges into being out of its opposite: *oubli.*

. . . ce qui nous rappelle le mieux un être,
c'est justement ce que nous avions oublié
(parce que c'était insignifiant, et que nous lui
avons ainsi laissé toute sa force). C'est pourquoi la meilleure part de notre mémoire est
hors de nous . . . Hors de nous? En nous pour
mieux dire, mais dérobée à nos propres regards,
dans un oubli plus ou moins prolongé. C'est
grâce à cet oubli seul que nous pouvons de
temps à autre retrouver l'être que nous fûmes,
nous placer vis-à-vis des choses comme cet être
l'était, souffrir à nouveau, parce que nous ne
sommes plus nous, mais lui, et qu'il aimait ce
qui nous est maintenant indifférent. (1 643 cf.
III 531n)

. . . what a person recalls to us most vividly is
precisely what we had forgotten, because it was
of no importance, and had therefore left in full
possession of its strength. That is why the better part of our memory exists outside ourselves. . . . Outside ourselves, did I say; rather
within ourselves, but hidden from our eyes in
an oblivion more or less prolonged. It is thanks
to this oblivion alone that we can from time to
time recover the creature that we were, range
ourselves face to face with past events as that
creature had to face them, suffer afresh because
we are no longer ourselves but he, and because
he loved what leaves us now indifferent. (1 488-
489)

And Proust is again explicit, at the beginning of the final sequence of recognitions. "Yes, if the remembered image, thanks to forgetting, has been unable to contract any link, to forge any connection between itself and the passing moment, if it has remained in place, in its time, if it has kept its distance, its isolation in the hollow of a valley or at the summit of a mountain, then it suddenly makes us breathe a fresh air, precisely because it is an air which one has breathed long ago . . . for true paradises are those which one has lost" (III 870/ II 994). Thanks to forgetting, then, the image can keep its purity, the singular quality it displays when set alongside the later image that evokes it. The twenty-year gap must be one of *oubli*—a blank, a hole in time, represented in Proust's novel by the undescribed time Marcel spent in three successive sojourns in a *maison de santé*. And what could be more appropriate? In other eras, a hole in time took the form of retirement to a monastery, languishing in a prison, banishment, or travel to a distant shore. But in the modern world of endless importunings and no escape, the only retirement is not physical but mental. Marcel simply withdraws into an unspecified condition of suspended life. In fact he states explicitly that he never was cured; it is as if he returns to life after the ritual period of time has elapsed. The *maison de santé* represents the *néant mental* of forgetfulness (I 821/I 618) in terms of a familiar institution.

We are perfectly justified then in saying that Proust-Marcel's phenomenal memory consisted in his capacity to forget in the intervals. "A man with a good memory," writes Samuel Beckett, "does not remember anything because he does not forget anything" (*Proust*, p. 17). Proust admitted to the Princesse Bibesco that "he had staked his life in a game of *qui-perd-gagne* [loser takes all]" (*Au bal avec Marcel Proust*, p. 121), and the paradox of memory-by-forgetting resembles just such a game.

Once we have become aware of the enormous role of *oubli* in determining the action of Proust's novel, we hold the key to other parts of his work that show *oubli* in different forms. The most important passages on sleep in A *la recherche* (1 821/1 618, II 84-91/772-79, 981-84/II 271-73) describe sleep as a forgetting, a foreshortening of time. It permits the reawakening of a purified individual who has lost himself and found himself again. And we are in effect perpetually asleep to most of ourselves until recognition or remembering brings a fragment of us back from *oubli*. Sleep reproduces daily and in miniature the whole rhythm of life: forgetting and self-recognition, death and resurrection. For *oubli* in the form of sleep places death beside us each night. The *maison de santé* represents an institutionalized, all-devouring form of sleep. And in the special universe of love *oubli* works in a particularly paradoxical fashion, for to forget a loved one leads both to indifference and to the possibility of renewed desire. Proust marked the following passage "capital" in the unfinished manuscript. "In this particular form *l'oubli*, though it worked to accustom me to separation from her, still, because it showed me a kinder and more beautiful Albertine, made me desire her return all the more" (III 461n/II 706).

Memory and forgetting in their close community of symbiosis carry us far into the vast realm of personality in Proust. I shall here confine myself to one brief observation on the subject. Marcel's lengthily examined "intermittences of heart" concerning the memory of his grandmother should be linked not to any inherent fickleness of disposition in him, but to a far different circumstance, often overlooked. "For our intermittences of heart are linked to the clouding [*troubles*] of our memory" (II 756/II 114). The sentence is as revealing as any in the whole novel. Probing beyond what Montaigne called inconstancy, Proust affirms that it is the natural pulse of our emotional and sentimental life to turn in a cycle, to forget large portions of itself in favor of others which come alive in turn and then fade again. And he follows Montaigne in not condemning this inconstancy but trying to track it to its source. The memory disturbance of *oubli* gives us Proust's version of the unconscious. Instead of hypostatizing a shadow mind as Freud does, Proust suggests very simply that we are and cannot help being self-forgetful. Applied thus to our subjective processes, Proust's structure of theories on time and forgetting, optics and memory, coincide with his presentation of personality as intermittent, unpredictable, contradictory. We cannot be all of ourselves all at once except in rare moments of self-recognition, as at the end of A *la recherche*. And those moments are essentially solitary. Conversely we cannot know the whole character of another person except by the intensified and comprehensive act of recognition that comes after prolonged absence. This too occurs only at the end of the novel. Therefore we go about most of the time in amazement at our own incapacity to recognize one another and ourselves, making out as best we can with habits and words, and blaming ourselves for being fickle. *Ainsi va le monde.*

As the novel form has developed beyond description of a deterministic environment toward probing the interior reality of the self, it has necessarily shifted its technique of presentation. The fetish of point of view in fiction corresponds to an awareness of the self as the source of meaning, of significance in experience. The style of writing known as stream of consciousness consists in pure point of view, no other order than that of the self struggling to reach the core of feeling (or to escape from it) in each successive moment. In Proust, however, the order is provided not by the mere lapse of events as in stream of consciousness manner but by an intermittent self-recognition. Chance encounters with earlier experience and their identification by memory provide means of reclaiming one's past, and the self gradually builds up like some highly intricate piece of crochet work—deeply woven back into itself. Inconstancy and fickleness very gradually give way to a pattern of recurrence.

In the light of what has been said so far, I want
now to go back and examine two of the best known
aspects of Proust's work: the *moments bienheureux*,
and—a subject as precise as the other is limitless—
the two opening sentences of *A la recherche*. I have
tried to summarize several pages of sprawling com-
mentary on the first subject in a diagram whose
schematic nature emphasizes several neglected
points.[7] Each of these *moments bienheureux* (also
referred to as *moments privilégiés* and *fétiches*, here
numbered to eleven by counting as one the five
successive experiences in the last volume) follows or
partially follows a uniform pattern. The pattern itself and the deviations from it give these moments
their particular feeling and significance. First, Marcel is always in a dispirited state of mind—bored,
usually tired, alone (or if not, annoyed by the presence of others interfering with his solitude), and
deeply entangled in the *train-train* of habitual living. Second, he experiences a physical sensation,
which comes unexpectedly and by chance through
any one of his senses or a complex of them, with no
one sense predominating throughout the book.
Third, the sensation is accompanied by a clear feeling of pleasure and happiness which far surpasses
anything explained by the sensation alone. These
three components, which occur together in the
present, combine in the fourth step to lift Marcel
steeply out of the present and raise him high
enough to see what he has lost sight of: an analo-
gous and forgotten event in the past. That event is
now remembered and recognized and assimilated

TABLE OF MOMENTS BIENHEUREUX (PRIVILEGIES) OR FETICHES

BASIC PATTERN

	1. state of mind	2. sensation	3. inner feeling	4. recognition of past (souvenir)	5. presentiment of future (avenir)	6. result

basic pattern results:

none
postponement
reflection
creation-vocation
entire book

I. Madeleine sequence (I 44-48/I 34-36)

1. "I was cold"; "weary"; "out of the ordinary"
2. "taste of tea and cake"; "I shuddered"
3. "exquisite pleasure"
4. "Sunday morning in Combray"; "the vast structure of recollection"
5. the entire book—"face to face with something that does not yet exist"; "I have to start ten times over"
6. ("The whole of Combray and its environs")

*II. The steeples of Martinville (I 179-82/I 138-40)

1. "beyond its ordinary limits"; "we went like the wind"; "in the absence of other company"
2. "sight of the twin steeples"; "lines moving in the sunshine"
3. "special pleasure"
4. ———
5. "reality foreshadowed" (cf. IV, X)
6. "I composed the following little fragment"

III. Smell in the little pavilion (I 492-94/I 376-77)

1. "I was in despair"
2. "chill and fusty smell"
3. "pleasure . . . rich with a lasting truth"; "exaltation"

4. Uncle Adolphe's little room (I 72/I 55)
5. (grandmother's attack) (II 309-11/I 936-38)

6. "I could not understand and postponed the attempt to discover why"

*IV. Three trees in Hudimesnil, near Balbec (I 717-19/I 543-45)

1. "I should have to be alone"
2. "three trees made a pattern"
3. "happiness like that at Martinville"

4. Martinville (cf. II)
5. "presentiment"; "if, in time, I should discover"

6. (the happiness "remained incomplete"; "I seemed to die unto myself")

V. Hawthorne bush, near Balbec (I 922/I 690)

1. (with Andrée)
2. "fretted and glossy leaves"
3. "touched to the heart"

4. Hawthorne in bloom at Combray
5. ——

6. ——

*VI. "Congealed memory" with Saint-Loup in Paris (II 396-98/I 1002-3)

1. "if I had remained alone"
2. "going down the stairs"; foggy night
3. "enthusiasm"

4. "vast patches of oblivion"; (Doncières, Combray, Rivebelle)
5. ——

6. ("wasted years through which I was yet to pass before that invisible vocation was to reveal itself")

TABLE OF MOMENTS BIENHEUREUX (PRIVILEGIES) OR FETICHES—*Continued*

*VII. "Kind of exaltation" after dinner at the Duke de Guermantes (II 547-49/I 1106-07)

1. "melancholy"; "carriage taking me to M. de Charlus' house"

2. "boring conversations . . . stories"

3. "I marvelled at my happiness"

4. ―――――

5. ―――――

6. "my exaltation subsided quickly"

VIII. "Disruption of my entire being" in the hotel at Balbec (II 755-60/II 113-16)

1. "cardiac exhaustion"

2. "touched the top button of my shoes"; "sobs . . . tears"

3. "felicity"; "grief"

4. "the face of my grandmother"; "I had just grasped that she was dead"

5. Marcel's own death; "I would be nothing"

6. ―――――
("For intermittances of heart are closely linked to disturbances of memory")

IX. Septet by Vinteuil (III 248-65/II 553-64)

1. "I was in an unknown country"

2. "a tender phrase, familiar and domestic, of the septet"; "the particular accent of that phrase"

3. "magic apparition"; "substantial joy"; "beginnings of a true life"

4. "sonata by Vinteuil"

5. "presentiment . . . of joy in the hereafter"

6. _____ (reflections on art and genius)

*X. "The train had halted out in the open country" (III 854-56/II 983-84)

1. "the thought of my lack of literary gifts"

2. "the sun . . . fell on a line of trees"

3. "not the slightest elation"; "absolute indifference"

4. _____

5. _____

6. _____

TABLE OF MOMENTS BIENHEUREUX (PRIVILEGIES) or FETICHES—*Continued*

XI. The reception at the house of the Prince de Guermantes (III 865-86/II 991-1005)
1. "the moment when all appears lost"

a. 2. "unevenly cut flagstones" (II 886-67/II 991-92) 3. "felicity"; "A deep azure intoxicated my sight"	4. Venice (III 623ff. / II 821ff.) 5.	
b. 2. "servant struck a spoon against a plate" (III 868/II 993) 3. "felicity"	4. "hammer of a trainman" (cf. X) 5.	
c. 2. "wiped my mouth with the napkin" (III 868/II 993) 3. "fresh vision of azure"	4. "first day of my stay at Balbec" 5.	6. reflections on the novel to come
d. 2. "harsh noise from a water pipe" (III 874/II 997) 3. "exstasy"; "ineffable vision"	4. "calls" from "pleasure boats off Balbec" 5.	
e. 2. *François le Champi*, book in the library (III 883-86) 3. "disagreeably stuck" (II 1004-05); "mystery of literature"; "a child arises"	4. "book my mother read aloud in Combray" 5.	

* Marcel is in motion: carriage, train, flight of stairs, etc.

into the same binocular field of vision with the present event.

The fifth part of this pattern is a little more subtle and has generally escaped notice even though it is essential to the full interpretation of these "landmarks" in Marcel's life and to the form of the novel itself. In the complete pattern, the first three components reach out to form a link not only with the past but also with an event or development *in the future*. At the close of the *madeleine* sequence "the whole of Combray" takes shape out of Marcel's teacup—not just the memory of the place but the yet to be composed narrative which completes that recollection. The *clochers de Martinville* look forward to the three trees near Balbec and to the line of poplars Marcel sees from the train on the way back to Paris. The musty odor in the little pavilion in the Champs-Elysées foreshadows the death of the grandmother. And the multiple sequence of *moments bienheureux* near the end reaches out, as a group, toward Marcel's final self-recognition as a person and writer. Proust's words *réalité préssentie* (1 178/1 138) explicitly state that in addition to backward looking recollection, these moments may look forward by presentiment to a related state of things in the future. Through this twin eyepiece Proust-Marcel can look out of the present at Time itself.

Depending now on the extent to which these five elements have been present and combined in a complete pattern—and frequently the pattern remains fragmentary or goes astray—a sixth element follows: some response to the experience. Four times the experience aborts and produces no results (V, VI, VII, X). Twice Marcel senses something he should reach out for beyond his present sensation, but he resigns himself to postponing the attempt (III, IV). Three times the narrator responds to the urging of the moment by a lengthy meditation on the nature of time, experience, life, and the most essential features of reality (VIII, IX, XI). Once the experience leads him to produce on the spot a literary text celebrating the moment, thus attaining an exhilarating sense of accomplishment (II). Once the experience is so complete *in retrospect* that its ultimate result can be calculated only in terms of the book itself (I).

Although they follow one basic pattern, therefore, the *moments bienheureux* are by no means repetitions and do not resemble identical eyelets through which to thread an unvarying experience of unconscious memory. In fact the fluctuations themselves take on unusual significance. After a promising start, the *moments bienheureux* fall off rapidly both in frequency and in intensity, until, at the end, a new impulsion revives them. A graph would look like this: ⌣⟋ . In the simplest of possible terms it represents the action of the book in profile. The low point in the curve, the dead point of all Proust's machinery, at which it seems incapable of moving again in spite of any force applied to it, comes at X when Marcel coldly confronts his lack of "any kind of elation" watching the line of obliquely lit poplar trees from the train (III 856/ II 984). But only thirty pages later, the sight of a novel by George Sand carries him beyond his mere memory to the power to recognize himself in the past. "That stranger was myself, he was the child I was then . . ." (III 884/II 1004).

This last of the *moments bienheureux* (which appears to have been inserted late in the text; see III 889, note 1/——) stands out in two respects among the five moments which come in rapid succession in these pages. It reaches all the way back to the beginning of the book, to the beginning of time in *la première abdication* at Combray. And secondly, the literary nature of this particular memory out of earliest family experiences gathers up and directs the flood of speculations about the novel which rises around the incident (III 879-916/II 1001-1028). In these magnificent pages on memory and forgetting, on death and the literary vocation, Marcel almost but not quite comes to final terms with himself. Proust might have closed the novel with Marcel's certainty (in quiet retreat in the Prince de Guermantes' library) that he now possesses the secret of recapturing the past and with his still unchallenged plan to apply this secret to a "new life" and the composition of a novel.

But it is not to be so. Marcel comes to terms with himself only one hundred and fifty pages and about an hour later, not in the evanescence of a sensation recalling his past, but in confronting the fine figure of a girl who by her exceptional birth reincarnates all the major characters of the story. Marcel's highly complex act of recognizing Mlle. de Saint-Loup demands as both its past and its future the novel itself—the one we have just read and the one Marcel will straightway set himself to write. This event alone, amplifying the feebler signal of the *madeleine* passage, establishes the pitch for the entire work of art, its living and writing.

But before we reach this ultimate moment, Proust insists that we make the transition. When the *maître d'hôtel* comes to tell Marcel in the library that he can enter the salon of the Prince de Guermantes, three highly significant pages turn the focus of the action away from the *moments bienheureux* toward the series of recognitions to follow (III 918-920/II 1029-1031). Though in the preceding meditations Marcel has distilled the "general essence" of involuntary memory, he now for the first time readies himself for "a new life that I had been unable to find in solitude" (III 918/II 1029). Many years and many pages of fragmentary experience have brought him everything except what he sought most of all: a life and a work. His time has come at last. Marcel steps into the prince's salon like an untried gladiator entering the arena for the first time. His sense of reality and identity undergoes a long series of assaults before he can win final certitude as an individual and an artist.

The entire theory of involuntary memory, released from the solitary and confining form of the *moments bienheureux* into the larger sphere of recognition and binocular vision in time, can now take us back to the opening of the book and one of the great enigmas of Proust. Not only has it never been solved; it has never been posed. Just how does one explain the syntax of the opening two sentences? No writer was ever so sensitive as Proust to the sheer tonus of tense in literary discourse. Marcel bursts into tears when he realizes he has spoken of his feelings for Gilberte in the past tense (1 633/1 481), just as in one of his few known love letters Proust focuses his passion on the tense in which he has to refer to the person he loves (*Disque vert*, 1953). And above all he spoke of the bewitching qualities of the imperfect tense. In Flaubert it "entirely changes the aspect of things and people, like a lamp which has been moved" (*Chroniques*, p. 199) and elsewhere: "I admit that a certain use of the imperfect indicative—of that cruel tense which presents life to us as something at the same time cruel and passive, which, in the very act of retracing our actions, turns them into illusion, buries them in the past without leaving us like the perfect tense the consolation of activity—has always remained for me an inexhaustible source of mystery and sadness" (*Pastiches et mélanges*, p. 239n).

Proust wrote his own novel predominantly in the imperfect tense, a condition which makes the pervading tone of sadness and illusion untranslatable into English. For we have no simple tense between the past (aorist) and the unwieldy progressive. Against the long lush undulating stretches of imperfect, the actions in Proust's novel requiring the *passé simple* stand out in startlingly clear silhouette. Marcel acts comparatively rarely, but his actions assume monumental proportions raised as they are out of that vast plateau of the imperfect— monumental, and sometimes so trivial and contrived as to carry us far into the domain of the comic. Through these two basic tenses, the present weaves a thread of generalized observation and permanent "truth" or "law." What then is one to make of the opening sentence, especially when one comes back to it after reading through the rest of the novel? Once one begins to consider the other possible versions of the same sentence, it appears deliberately to avoid the characteristic tenses of the novel, the imperfect, the *passé simple*, the present.

Longtemps, je me suis couché de bonne heure.

Why did Proust not clarify his meaning with a temporal preposition or follow conventional syntax?

Depuis longtemps, je me couche de bonne heure.
Depuis longtemps, je me couchais de bonne heure.
Longtemps, je me couchai de bonne heure.
Longtemps, je me couchais de bonne heure.

There are arguments against all four. The first, moving directly into the present, begins to sound confessional and familiar. The second tends to anticipate a specific event coming along to break the routine suggested by the imperfect. The third throws the whole action into the remote past. The fourth—probably the least distorted and the version which is usually understood (and translated) instead of the inscrutable sentence Proust actually wrote—yields too quickly to the pull of reminiscence. Is the sentence, as written, merely conversational and casual in its choice of tense? I doubt it. May we conclude that Proust wanted to keep this opening sentence free of any exact location in time and to begin in a temporal free zone? In part this is surely the effect, whether deliberate or not. A *la recherche* begins outside of time, or hovering above it, and it will end by climbing back up to this altitude. But if we look and listen long enough, this sentence suddenly reveals a deeper secret in the heart of its verbal construction. *Longtemps*: a period of indefinite duration at any point in time. Then: *je me suis couché. Passé composé.* Not a simple tense but a compound tense composed of two other tenses, or times (*temps* meaning both tense and time in French). The French language, like English, contains a verb form which crosses the present of the auxiliary with the past of the participle to form what we curiously call the perfect—a past action still working its effect in the present and not yet separated from us by insignificance or temporal remoteness. *Two* times then, past and present, locked in the compound verb form, a fact which allows us to perceive in this, the first verb of the novel, the double time sense of the entire work. Marcel is in bed both literally in the past and symbolically-grammatically in the present as he tells of it—an indefinite time spanning past and present, *passé indéfini* as it is also called. Without this interpretation, the first sentence remains annoyingly vague

and amorphous; with it, these eight words embody
the mood and significance of the three thousand
pages to follow, because of the very fact that they
do not employ one of the simple tenses out of
which the rest of the book is gradually constructed.
We can read fully into the depths of this opening
sentence only when we have finished the novel and
have plumbed Marcel's past and present here
crossed in a syntactic equivalent of temporality.

The syntax of Proust's opening sentence (with
its two words for time) subsumes the movement of
the entire novel in another way. Neither transitive,
bringing its action to bear on another part of the
universe, nor intransitive, arresting any direct effect
in mid-flight, the verb is reflexive. The subject turns
softly around to discover itself in a new guise: the
"accusative"! Extending from here, the action of the
book takes place within Marcel himself multiplied
into different reflexive and accusative persons. The
reflexiveness, the monumental circular subjectivity
of *A la recherche*, as a whole, philosophically and
psychologically and even syntactically, forms a subject unto itself, beginning with the first sentence.
The passage quoted on page 15 reproduces the circular movement on the scale of a lengthy paragraph
turning back to surprise itself: "Why it's you!" And
the self-recognition I have proposed as the central
theme of the book constitutes a totally reflexive action. What the full novel unfolds is the experience
and the *oubli* that comes to separate the *je* from the
me before they reunite—what lodges between I
and me. Most written languages contain an equiva-

lent of the revealing expressions: "I forgot myself," and "I came to myself." Proust's "A long time, I lay me down to sleep at an early hour," begins a self-forgetfulness that will last until a coming-to, a novel and a lifetime later.

Only once again does Proust require his syntax to embody his time doctrine in this precise fashion. In the *madeleine* sequence, after Marcel's vain attempts to identify the source of his pleasurable sensations the dénouement of the incident comes unexpectedly in a sentence parallel to the one I have been examining. "Et tout d'un coup le souvenir m'est apparu" (1 46/1 36). And then the final sentence of this opening section: ". . . tout Combray . . . est sorti . . . de ma tasse de thé" (1 48/ 1 36). Here, forty pages later, the effect is reinforced. We sense that the memory is with him as he writes, conferring on him the power to compose the novel. Such a device, however, cannot be used often without extinguishing its effect. The *passé composé* does not occur again with this stereoscopic significance.

IV

Proust's sensitivity to time and tense must not draw our attention permanently away from other aspects of his work that give it body and variety. Particularly I want to insist on how fully he assimilated into his universe of vision two perspectives often treated as merely decorative or even out of place. The first is Proust's sense of the comic. His masterful handling of realistic detail gives us an insight into every social level, be it Francoise's *cuirs* or the Guermantes' so-called wit. The slow motion scene of Marcel "kissing" Albertine (II 363-67/I 977-81) is as right and as ridiculous as Mme. Cottard falling helplessly asleep after dinner (II 960/II 256). A form of the comic more basic to the book appears in the recurring pattern of mistaken identities. More than any comedy by Plautus with two sets of identical twins as its principal characters, *A la recherche* advances through an arsenal of disguises which, before they serve as the means of revealing partial truths, provide us with sustained comic diversion. But the largest dimension of comic meaning in Proust's novel concerns the very progression of the action in a manner only too easy to overlook. The whole first portion of Combray concerning his *tante* Léonie, is embroidered around a minor matter of local interest: Did Mme. Goupil arrive at mass before the elevation? Léonie, from her ringside seat on village life, becomes obsessed by the question and then forgets completely to find out the answer from her only sure source of information, Eulalie. This trivial yet imperious question, from which hangs a whole day of her existence (and fifty pages of the novel along with it [I 55-109/I 42-83]), leads us into the churning of Léonie's subjective processes. And exactly this process of tumor-like growth lodges at the base of Swann's prolonged jealousy over Odette: Had Forcheville been with her the day she had not answered the door? Two whole volumes of the novel spin themselves out over Marcel's self-torture about the possibility of Albertine's having indulged her lesbian inclinations. The ludicrous resides next door to the serious. The most crucial and passionate concerns of our existence, after having produced a condition of elephantiasis in our inner thoughts, dwindle to nothing, like a comic shadow. Throughout the book many of the most serious moments and the most earnest theoretical discussions push our sense of the incongruity of events to the point where laughter is the only possible reaction. At the open-

ing of the last scene in the prince's salon, the scene
which is going to bring him the final grasp of truth,
Marcel says gaily of M. d'Argencourt, fallen into
senile decay: "I had a crazy laugh at this sublime
dotard [*gaga*]" (III 922/II 1032). The remark spans
the entire comic perspective of magnified realism,
mistaken identity, and obsession; it is not plastered
over the surface of the book as decoration but pene-
trates to its basic structure and composition.

Alongside this deep-running comedy, another
powerful perspective lends coherence to the immensity of Proust's work. In the uniqueness and incon-
sistency of the particular, Proust's intelligence perpetually seeks a hidden order. He speaks without
hesitation of "psychological laws" and uses numerous scientific metaphors such as "moral chemistry"
(III 585/II 794) to suggest that men as much as things
obey the workings of universal law. The entire apparatus of optical figures applied to our conscious
and unconscious faculties as well as to social history
implies that a set of laws forming a coherent science
can describe these human processes. For the most
part Proust avoids classifications that delimit individual behavior in favor of generalizations that discover a regularity and coherence within a state of
perpetual change. He had the scientist's and moral-
ist's sense of law as something exciting and alive,
and many times his patient, probing intelligence
seems to partake of the genius of Fabre and La
Rochefoucauld and Poincaré.

Encouraged by Proust's own remarks in many
texts on the comparative importance of "sensibility"

and "intelligence" in his work, critics have hotly de-
bated the role of laws and generalizations as a form
of knowledge and as an element of art in A *la
recherche*. Some critics maintain that Proust's high-
est accomplishment lay in his capacity to shape
highly original generalizations about human conduct
into a work of fiction that brings them to life. A more
numerous group object to the undeniable rational
strain in Proust's writing and confine their admiration to his highly developed poetic sensibility before
nature, before his own subjective processes, and
before the illusory nature of our relations with
others. Proust himself can be quoted at length and
tellingly in support of both attitudes and in oppo-
sition to them. In the closing pages of "Combray,"
when Marcel is losing hope of ever becoming a
writer, he speaks of the "particular pleasure" of
certain sensations and of his ignorance of their significance. With heavy irony he depicts his youthful
ignorance in equating literature with intelligence:
"It was not impressions of that sort, surely, that
were able to restore my lost hope of one day being a
writer and a poet, for they were all linked to a
particular object of no intellectual value and led to
no abstract truth" (1 179/1 137). The remarks sur-
rounding most of the *moments bienheureux* include
a comparable disparagement of rational processes;
Contre Sainte-Beuve opens with the uncompromis-
ing sentence, "Every day I attach less value to the
intelligence" (p. 53). Nevertheless, Proust has to
admit in the same volume that Nerval, though
"there is a little too much intelligence in what he

writes," embodied into the "masterpiece" *Sylvie*
the same six or seven "laws of thought" that
Proust had counted up (p. 168). Certain passages in
A la recherche sound more like the pronouncements
of a nineteenth-century determinist than of a twen-
tieth-century poet. "Thus it is useless to observe
social behavior, for one can deduce it all from
psychological laws" (I 513/I 392). ". . . Anything
really important for a man can happen only in spite
of him, by the action of some great natural law"
(II 160/I 829). And in the end, viewed with just a
little objectivity, even the highly particularized and
seemingly exceptional world Proust-Marcel has been
describing dwindles into a pattern very close to
typical.

> Mais si je sortais de moi et du milieu qui
> m'entourait immédiatement, je voyais que ce
> phénomène social n'était pas aussi isolé qu'il
> m'avait paru d'abord et que du bassin de Com-
> bray où j'étais né, assez nombreux en somme
> étaient les jets d'eau qui symétriquement à moi
> s'étaient élevés au-dessus de la même masse
> liquide qui les avait alimentés. (III 968)

> But if I looked beyond myself and my immedi-
> ate environment, I saw that this social phenom-
> enon was not as isolated as it had at first ap-
> peared to me and that, from the Combray
> basin where I was born, quite numerous after
> all were the fountains that had risen sym-
> metrically with myself above the liquid mass
> which had fed them all. (II 1067)

Chosen for the purpose, one's quotes can prove pretty much what one wants about the role of law and intelligence in *A la recherche*—a fact which usually reduces any discussion of the question to confusion. Furthermore, many of Proust's "laws" appear far more the fruit of an intuitive process than of systematic observation and induction. But Proust's work shows that he was not unaware of his ambivalent attitude toward human rational powers and he made it one of the themes of his work. Marcel vacillates in his feelings toward his own intelligence very much as he vacillates in his affection for Gilberte and Mme. de Guermantes and Albertine. The early portions of the book generally favor sentiment; increasingly toward the end, reason is admitted to an important place alongside sentiment and complementing it. A highly "reasonable" passage toward the end of the novel—probably added late in its composition yet now a part of its texture provides a full description of the perspective of intelligence of generalization within the larger optic of memory or recognition.

> . . . de ce que l'intelligence n'est pas l'instrument le plus subtil, le plus puissant, le plus approprié pour saisir le vrai, ce n'est qu'une raison de plus pour commencer par l'intelligence et non par un intuitivisme de l'inconscient, par une foi aux pressentiments toute faite. C'est la vie qui, peu à peu, cas par cas, nous permet de remarquer que ce qui est le plus important pour notre coeur, ou pour notre esprit,

ne nous est pas appris par le raisonnement,
mais par des puissances autres. Et alors, c'est
l'intelligence elle-même qui, se rendant compte
de leur supériorité, abdique, par raisonnement,
devant elles, et accepte de devenir leur colla-
boratrice et leur servante. Foi expérimentale.
(III 423)

. . . the fact that our intellect is not the most
subtle, the most powerful, the most appropriate instrument for grasping the truth, is only a
reason the more for beginning with the intellect, and not with a subconscious intuition, a
ready-made faith in presentiments. It is life
that, little by little, case by case, enables us to
observe that what is most important to our
heart, or to our mind, is learned not by reason-
ing but by other powers. And then it is the intellect itself which, taking note of their superi-
ority, abdicates its sway to them upon reasoned
grounds and consents to become their collabo-
rator and their servant. It is faith confirmed by
experiment. (II 678)

The intelligence with its capacity to discrimi-
nate and to generalize can be a faithful guide along
the path to discovery; or, as Proust writes in *Contre
Sainte-Beuve*, "For if intelligence does not merit the
supreme crown, still only intelligence is capable of
bestowing it" (p. 59). Without an "experimental
faith" in this faculty, we shall not work up to
the subtler and higher faculties which combine images without recourse to laws. This passage defines

the fullness of Proust-Marcel's attitude toward human faculties more clearly than the better-known page (III 898/II 1015) which states that the truths of the intelligence "enchase" the higher truths of certain sensations recreated out of time. The role of the intelligence is not to decorate, but point out the route along which one can find the higher vision. Thus I take exception to Albert Feuillerat's conclusion about the word *enchâsser:* "this word defines precisely the kind of work Proust devoted himself to in revising his first draft" (*Comment Proust a composé son roman,* p. 249). Quite the contrary: in so far as Proust did add pages of analysis and generalization to the earlier "poetic" version of his novel (and Feuillerat quite understandably overstates his thesis) he was not just drawing in useless arabesques, but filling in the stages by which a mature person as contrasted to a child or adolescent reaches the "Proustian vision."

The relation of intelligence to intuition, of law to consciousness and "free will" becomes one of the most crucial questions in all the great novelists whose ambition drove them to portray both the life of an era and an individual attitude toward life. Stendhal and Tolstoy display deeply divided loyalties similar to Proust's, and this circumstance seems to have something to do with the novel as a form, as an order of magnitude for experience. In *De l'amour,* Stendhal affirms at the start that he is going to give us "an exact and scientific description of a kind of madness very rare in France." Naturally the book becomes less and less systematic until it devolves into a series of fragments and appendices. Stendhal's point of view in his novels and even his journals alternates between passionate abandonment to his characters and detachment from them in order to reduce them to a pattern of behavior. Tolstoy is driven by a comparable alternating current. He sets up and defends inflexible laws of history and morality, yet the individuality of his greatest characters from Kutuzov to Ivan Ilych lies in their grasp of these laws not by reason but by feeling, by intuition. Both Stendhal and Tolstoy show a strong inclination to cinch a demonstration by putting it into military terms—or better yet, mathematical terms, as if this latter form were truly irrefutable. (Tolstoy gives us equations for measuring military morale. In *Henri Brulard* Stendhal justifies his love for mathematics because it "does not admit hypocrisy and vagueness, my two pet aversions.") But the point is that both, like Proust, erect an extensive edifice of law and intelligence in order to abandon it when the occasion arises. The secret is to know when to abdicate the categories of reason for a higher, more mysterious, and more hazardous faculty. Or—and the question must finally be asked—do the two commonly separated sets of terms for intelligence and sensibility stand for different settings and yields of a single mental process rather than for two opposed processes? I pass, as Proust passed; the question remains.

I wonder, in fact, if Proust's searching and cryptic term in the last quotation, "experimental faith," does not refer to a process related to Keats' "negative capability." Keats wished to dwell "in uncertainties, Mysteries, doubts, without any irritable reaching after fact and reason." But whereas Keats as a poet sought to maintain a pure state of selfless response to the world around him without being bound by the categories of personality and intelligence, the three novelists accept such a state as exceptional, the rare moment of elevation we may experience, if we are able, under proper circumstances, to break free from habits of thought. By which I do not mean to suggest that Proust and Stendhal and Tolstoy were disappointed poets unable to keep the spirit in flight. They observed an essentially human mode of existence: the intermittent rhythm of awareness they depict swings between laws of behavior and moments of pure uninhibited freedom and insight. This double mode of existence arises from the most fundamental condition of man, his dual nature—or at least his dual grasp of his nature. Stendhal's obsession with love, Tolstoy's with history, and Proust's with memory allow them to investigate along converging paths the very beat of life. The soaring of a poem by Keats represents a single unsullied act. The novel in the hands of these three epic authors records a long series of moments on different levels of intensity. This order of magnitude encompasses many moods, many mansions.

Both the perspective of comedy (alternating with seriousness) and the perspective of law (alternating with pure sensibility) tell us a great deal about Proust's mind and about the unity of his novel. But I should contend that they do not reveal quite so much as the handful of optical principles that describe how Proust's vision influenced the nature of his art, the form of his fiction. How, specifically, does the combination of slightly dissimilar images, the essential role of interval and forgetting, bear on the form of *A la recherche*? The answer, though lengthy, is revealing.

The opening reverie of the book gradually focuses on the one vivid scene Marcel can recall from his childhood: being deprived of his mother's goodnight kiss. The unexpected spell of the *madeleine* experience suddenly enlarges the narrow aperture of his memory to reveal the whole of Combray—the place and the era. Marcel's secure and almost unstained vision of the world as something whose existence he could believe in as it appears to him, begins to waver only when he tries to fix it at the end in a fragmentary work of art—the description he writes of seeing the *clochers de Martinville* from the carriage. After these two hundred pages of overture, the aperture of Marcel's memory enlarges even further to include the story of his older friend and alter ego, Swann, and then opens so wide as to disappear in the total recall of his own past. But these twenty-six hundred pages pick up every whisper and shadow of perverseness and corruption in the overture and pursue them relentlessly, until we have been plunged into a universe characterized by total disorder, unintelligibility, and disintegration of all values. Only in the last two hundred pages will the pieces be fitted together again: but not exactly as in the beginning. For what intervenes has not been a mere diversion. The body of the novel consists in a prolonged series of false answers which Marcel follows with pathetic enthusiasm: sentimental love, the allurement of aristocratic society, the desire for fame, friendship. They all turn out to be "inevitable disappointments" (I 874/I 656). The action of the novel reproduces on a large scale the "deceptive" presentation Proust pointed out in Dostoevsky's treatment of character (III 378-81/ II 644-46). After the opening, we venture out into the wide world in Marcel's company on a long series of false scents, each of which is followed into an impasse. In the bulk of the incidents of the novel he comes up against false answers to the basic questions of life.

Love is selfish and self-deluding. Elegant society is a sham and dupes no one so completely as its own initiates. Celebrity corrupts a man until he becomes an unbearable travesty of himself. Friendship too is suspect. The only thing Marcel sees clearly once he has lost his pristine vision, is the perverse incapacity of men to experience life directly, face to face. Our "moral perspective" prevents us from enjoying pleasure when we attain it and sets us yearning after any mysterious absent being that tantalizes our desire. The surest thing about people is their perverseness and the instability of their desires (III 460/II 705). Conversely, "Time passes, and little by little every falsehood spoken becomes true . . ." (III 461/II 706). And thus it happens that any partial interpretation of Proust's work, based primarily on the beginning and middle sections, falls into irretrievable error. So intelligent a critic as Denis Saurat has tried to show Proust's world as one of sensuous pleasure and illness, a picture as incomplete as an attempt to interpret the Christian religion without taking into account the resurrection.

Most of *A la recherche* moves negatively along false scents, backwards into the future as I have suggested earlier. I can say the same thing now in an optical figure and thus relate this aspect of the book to much of what has been said so far. Marcel and the reader, after the opening glimpse of paradise in Combray, move on into the world with only one eye open. Relief in time, binocular vision of reality, come only in moments of mysterious pleasure provoked by an unfamiliar setting (carriage, train, hotel) or by music. Then suddenly at the end, the other eye opens when we are sure it has atrophied, and Marcel attains both the wholeness of vision to recognize himself and his world, and the final certainty of his vocation. Snobbery, physical desire, egotistical perverseness—all these are aspects of an incomplete vision of the world seen with one eye open. And Proust obliges us to see in that limited fashion for a long time. The novel, in retrospect, begins to take on the appearance of a game of twenty questions, all but the last of which elicit a negative answer; or a detective story, in which every clue leads to a blind alley until an unforeseeable insight recombines them all into the solution.

And we now confront a perfectly legitimate yet rarely asked question, which applies not only to Proust but to every tale of quest and long-delayed discovery. Why take twenty-six hundred pages to narrate in great detail and vividness all Marcel's missteps and false conclusions? Why present us with so magnificent a construction of the erroneous universe from which the true time dimension is missing? The answer delves toward the very foundations of the novel as a form of art, the novel, which is always to some degree—though usually less massively than A *la recherche*—a tissue of errors. The kind of loose narrative we have come to call the novel rests on error both as to its esthetics and the source of its moral tone. Because we are what we are, habit-ridden and perverse, the false scent or the one-eyed vision of things will at first lead us closer to true knowledge and insight than will full divulgence. We remain immobilized until we confront and fully comprehend our mistakes. Swann cannot at first believe that the Vinteuil he knew in Combray could possibly be the composer with the same name who wrote the sonata. Later this association reinforces his admiration for the music. In the famous scene relating Marcel's discovery of Charlus' true biological identity, Proust forces us to relate the recognition of truth to error. After mentioning that "Ulysses himself did not recognize Athena at first," the paragraph concludes: "An error, when dissipated, gives us an additional sense" (II 613/II 12). And later we read, "This perpetual error which is precisely 'life,' does not bestow its thousand forms merely upon the visible and the audible universe but upon the social universe, the sentimental universe, the historical universe, and so forth" (III 573-74/II 785). Error, optical illusion, provides the material out of which truth must emerge, as evolution must emerge out of the regression and elimination of many species.

But *emerge* is as vague a word as the language possesses for so crucial a process, biological, moral, or esthetic. Emerge how? The biologist can give us a fairly convincing description of natural selection. In his ambitious work *Space, Time and Deity* the philosopher S. Alexander offers a somewhat less convincing description of "emergent" deity, the next evolutionary step for man. What happens in the novel is much closer to us than either of these, a process Proust carried to the extreme of length and intensity. Throughout the central portion of *A la recherche*, the dominant attitude of Marcel before the world is summed up in the deceptively simple phrase, "cet immense désir de connaître la vie" (III 553/II 770). But matched in an apparently losing struggle against this curiosity, which ranges from the innocent to the morbid, Marcel shows a deeply ingrained idealism: "I preferred that life should be on a level with my intuitions" (III 610/II 810). Both these remarks are made in connection with Marcel's obsessive desire to learn the "truth" about Albertine's life and character; he discovers no truth, only a cryptic sequence of falsehoods. Truth and reality in Proust have no objective, verifiable existence. They are the esthetic creations of our intuitions, of our minds, fixed in a work of art. Therefore it is by an act of creation that truth "emerges" from deception and illusion. Marcel's vision of truth and his sense of vocation occur as one "recognition" in the novel, for they are merely different aspects of the same process of creating our world. We must ourselves create the truth of existence insofar as we can recognize its pattern and relief in time; and in the same way we truly create ourselves, our character, by a long and often delayed act of self-recognition. The moral and esthetic meanings are thus fused in a concept of self-creation very close to what we have become familiar with in statements of existentialist conviction. In *L'Etre et le néant* and later works, Sartre assembles a whole battery of special terms (*imagination, assomption, transcendance, être-pour-soi*) to describe this mysterious emergence out of ourselves. We are what we turn ourselves into. In order to make anything of ourselves, we first follow a long path of error, our own particularized error. For Proust-Marcel there are twenty-six hundred pages of it.

Thus Proust's literary and moral construction in *A la recherche*, which approaches truth obliquely along the false scent of error, has brought us inexorably to the question of the length of the novel. Proust wrote voluminously—so much so, some readers feel, that he suffocates us in his brilliant portrait of the iniquity of man. We come close to losing any sense of uprightness or integrity in human beings. But having once grasped the basic structure of his novel around 1909 or 1910, Proust never shrank from the enormous dimensions such a concept demanded. In 1919 he wrote to Paul Souday, "My composition is veiled and its outline only gradually perceptible because it unfolds on so vast a scale" (*Correspondance générale*, III 69). In his article on Flaubert, he extends the figure when he refers to the "rigorous composition" of the first volume of his own novel as "difficult to discern because drawn with the compass legs wide apart and because the section that corresponds to an earlier section, cause and effect, are located at a great distance from one another" (*Chroniques*, p. 210). Sheer mass was an essential element of his art and he resolved not to sacrifice it. "The writer may embark upon a long work without apprehension" (III 907/II 1021). In a letter to the editor of *Les Annales* in 1921, defending himself against charges of writing a purely analytical novel, he states he wants to subject reality "to the least possible shrinkage."

There is another important consideration, closely related to the esthetic of the false scent, that explains this resoluteness before the task of composing a novel of vast dimensions. Proust wrote at length in order to create within the frame of his novel an interval of *oubli*, the forgetting which would allow the reader a true experience of remembering and recognizing. This contention runs a great critical risk, for it appears equivalent to saying that to describe anger or boredom one should write in an angry or boring fashion, and so on. But Proust's style is in no way forgetful, nor is he describing *oubli*; he is reproducing it as a speech in a play reproduces anger. He dramatizes forgetting and memory and recognition in a prolonged monologue which need not stop to describe what it most simply *is*. Proust recreates his compound vision of the world in a metaphor so extended we forget the first term and then recall it. Just as in "Combray" we forget the narrative thread of Mme. Goupil being late to Mass, in the full work we, like Marcel himself, have forgotten many of the characters by the time they reappear in the last scene. So much wealth of experience cannot be carried along perpetually on the surface of our minds.

Twice, Proust hints at the relation between the length of his narrative and the importance he attributes to *oubli*. Just at the end of his meditations, before entering the prince's salon, Marcel mentions having recently leafed through several novels of Bergotte, first read long ago, in order to see how they end.

> Car je ne me rappelais plus bien ce qui était arrivé à ces personnages, ce qui ne les différenciait d'ailleurs pas des personnes qui se trouvaient cet après-midi chez Mme. de Guermantes et dont, pour plusieurs au moins, la vie passée était aussi vague pour moi que si je l'eusse lue dans un roman à demi oublié. (III 914)

> For I no longer remembered just what happened to these characters—in which, moreover, they resembled the persons who were at Mme. de Guermantes' this afternoon and whose past life, in several cases at least, was as vague in my

mind as if I had read it in some half-forgotten novel. (II 1026)

The "half-forgotten novel" is no mere figure: it lies under our eyes and is approaching its climax, a novel which shades off into a misty past like our own lives and our own experience. This existence in depth begins to reveal the very essence of Proust, a multi-dimensionality that could never be conveyed by an epigram or even a short story. And a few pages later Marcel realizes his attainment to a "new life" no longer depends on a condition of solitude:

. . . (comme j'avais cru autrefois, comme cela avait peut-être été pour moi autrefois, comme cela aurait peut-être dû être encore si je m'étais harmonieusement développé, au lieu de ce long arrêt qui semblait seulement prendre fin). (III 918)

. . . as I had formerly believed and as had perhaps formerly been true in my case and might, perhaps, have still been true if I had developed in a uniform manner, without that long suspension of activity which seemed to be only just coming to an end. (II 1029)

The long "arrest" in his development between the opening and the close of the novel, his years of wandering in the labyrinth of delusion, again turn out to be the very force which bring him face to face with the true life. That wandering in the desert, to have its full effect in a work of literature as Proust conceived it, must be reproduced and re-created in the body of the narrative. Only after establishing this life-sized scale of events did Proust allow himself to state flatly that "many years passed" before Marcel left the *maison de santé;* he has earned the right to that abbreviation of narrative.

The dimensions of Proust's novel, however, though grandiose in their original conception and execution as offered for publication in 1912, almost tripled in length during the ten years which followed. There is a famous culinary legend about the *chef cuisinier* of Napoleon III, who discovered he had put his potatoes into deep fat too soon for the emperor's arrival. Anxiously he took them out, gambling his reputation in the process, and plunged them back in at the last moment to complete the cooking. In so doing, and to his everlasting glory, he discovered *pommes soufflées,* one of the greatest delicacies the humble potato can yield. After the not very successful publication of the first volume in 1913, the serving up of Proust's novel was similarly delayed by the circumstance of war. What began appearing again seven years later bears a certain relation to a literary *pomme soufflée.* The size and scope of the novel had been blown up enormously, even though the basic ingredients and structure had not changed. And it is my contention that for the reasons just given concerning scale of narration, Proust thus improved his novel and produced a work of art more forceful and original in its significance than the first version.

This conviction brings me once again up

against the critic Feuillerat, who takes an opposite position. After stating that the opening and, for the most part, the conclusion of *A la recherche* stayed in place through all modifications, he concludes: "But everything in between has been violently and irretrievably dislocated, and without our being able to discover the tiniest constructive intent in the way the additions were inserted" (*Comment Marcel Proust a composé son roman*, p. 255). A few pages later he takes Proust to task both for abandoning the clarity of his original chronology and for adding generalizations which "déchirerent à tout instant l'atmosphère de rêve éveillé" (p. 262). Feuillerat's sense of loss over the lineaments of the original that have been buried or mutilated in the new prevents him from perceiving what has been gained, indeed what *adds* to the atmosphere of a waking dream. For dislocation is exactly the word to describe the mood and "logic" of dream. The original tripartite structure of the book, with its two ends anchored in involuntary memory and self-recognition, was sturdy enough to bear a great deal more length and weight in the middle. And its progression, which rests not on an unbroken chronological sequence as Feuillerat mistakenly thought but on an interruption (*arrêt*) and transposition of time onto a higher level, could tolerate the interposition of great chunks of narrative—even some of inferior literary quality. But these additions allow us a deeper perspective on the story because of the wider spacing of the images finally combined. The sheer length creates *oubli*, materializes into a long literary excursion the postponement of Marcel's vocation, and heightens the effect of revelation and reversal at the end. Proust's additions, the product in part of intelligent generalization as well of youthful revery, combine to expand the time or space (both apply) of the novel in which his "psychology in time" can unfold. Moreover, the twisting of many asides and subordinate incidents into a single though sometimes tangled strand of text, gives the book the texture of something that has aged as a person or a tree ages, suggesting a past as well as a present and recording in its appearance the stress of experience in many weathers. It is the result of an author's unflagging dedication to a single work—the gnarled, sturdy, and cross-grained sense of reality we discover in Montaigne's *Essays*, in Baudelaire's *Les Fleurs du mal*, and in Whitman's *Leaves of Grass*. More than any of these others, Proust followed an all-encompassing structure, often referred to in musical composition as ABA. He extended it to the utmost by prolonging the B section to the point where we forget A. But in that temporary masking or camouflaging of the structure without destroying it lies a remarkable achievement of the book. The second A, *Le temps retrouvé*, rises up suddenly like the genie from his bottle, when we least expect him.

The dimensions of the novel, then, the aspect which makes it difficult to grasp it in its entirety and to approach it with conventional critical concepts of unity or the transitoriness of poetic inspiration, work a transformation upon our experience which could not be fully conveyed in any other fashion. When, in the closing pages, Proust seeks to bring this vastness closer to the individual reader, to make him feel more at home with its immensity, he turns us back to look not at the novel but *through* it at the world and ourselves.

> En réalité, chaque lecteur est, quand il lit, le propre lecteur de soi-même. L'ouvrage de l'écrivain n'est qu'une espèce d'instrument optique qu'il offre au lecteur afin de lui permettre de discerner ce que, sans ce livre, il n'eût peut-être pas vu en soi-même. (III 911)

> In reality, each reader reads only what is already within himself. The book is only a sort of optical instrument which the writer offers to the reader to enable the latter to discover in himself what he would not have found but for the aid of the book. (II 1024)

> . . . mon livre n'étant qu'une sorte de ces verres grossissants comme ceux que tendait à un acheteur l'opticien de Combray; mon livre, grâce auquel je leur fournirais le moyen de lire en eux-mêmes. (III 1035)

> . . . my book serving merely as a sort of magnifying glass, such as the optician of Combray used to offer to a customer, so that through my book I would give them the means of reading in their own selves. (II 1113)

Bientôt je pus montrer quelques esquisses [de mon oeuvre]. Personne n'y comprit rien. Même ceux qui furent favorables à ma perception des vérités que je voulais ensuite graver dans le temple, me félicitèrent de les avoir découvertes au "microscope," quand je m'étais au contraire servi d'un téléscope pour apercevoir des choses, très petites en effet, mais parce qu'elles étaient situées à une grande distance, et qui étaient chacune un monde. (III 1041)

Soon I was able to shew a few sketches. No one understood a word. Even those who were favorable to my conception of the truths which I intended later to carve within the temple congratulated me on having discovered them with a microscope when I had, on the contrary, used a telescope to perceive things which, it is true, were very small but situated afar off and each of them a world in itself. (II 1118)

Telescopes, yes, but bi- or multi-ocular: on this I insist over and above Proust's apt images. For *A la recherche* provides us with an image combined out of many images, a stereoscopic re-creation of the world in depth.

Usually when we look at a novel, we see a set of characters enacting a series of events and gradually achieving reality as personalities. Proust, having accomplished this in greater relief than had ever been attempted before, proceeded to turn his machinery back toward life, toward himself. He created a transparent novel, a set of characters who, once created, disappear and leave us the limpidity of an optical glass. The earliest remarks on the novel in A la recherche center around the "opaque" quality of real people contrasted with the "immateriality" of a novelist's imaginary creations, permitting us to see into the latter (185/164). Marcel carries this immateriality even further by simply vanishing from the scene after meeting Mlle. de Saint-Loup. The action moves abruptly to another level, and the sentiments of respect or indulgence or spite toward Marcel felt by the characters resurrected in the last scene are left behind. Marcel withdraws into pure consciousness for the last fifteen pages, becomes a transparent subjectivity addressing itself to a work of art. This concluding self-effacement of Marcel as a person in any realistic or novelistic sense gives the book its quality of being less an object of our vision than an optical medium or instrument that modifies and directs our vision. As a novel, A la recherche finally jettisons any story and changes into a device for beholding and transmuting life, Proust's, our own, everyone's. The most recent, painstaking, and literal minded of Proust's biographers, George D. Painter, calls A la recherche "a creative autobiography" in which, "though he invented nothing, he altered everything." (Proust: The Early Years, p. xiii) But such a point of view can be taken only after reading the book through as fiction and following its own interior transformation into a reflection back on life and truth.

Just what do we see, looking back at life through

the lens of Proust's novel? Many things, that are in the end one thing. First of all it is worth insisting—particularly in view of the bowdlerized English translation of the title, *Remembrance of Things Past*, to which Proust himself objected strongly—that the novel does not simply relate a pleasant stroll down memory lane to find the redolent memoirs of an era. After its complicated chronological preliminaries, the novel *moves forward* in time even though the action in its psychological and social preoccupations *faces the past*. The narrative tone that results, composed of sudden apparitions and gradual disappearances, hauntingly recalls the view from the rear platform of an old-fashioned observation car. There one always felt a faint wistful vertigo produced by this backward advance into the future out of a diminishing past. Thus in Proust we travel through the age of names and of places, and on across the wider expanses of the age of loves and the age of laws. Only at the end do we gain release from this restricted outlook in which life appears to be a perpetual dwindling of experience, and reach a higher view, the "special sense" whose "application" Proust considered the origin of his book (*Correspondance générale*, III 194).

We have been carefully prepared for this special sense from the beginning. The opening pages of "Combray" contain it implicitly in the wavering state of mind which characterizes Marcel's *drame du coucher*. His only consolation on going to bed is his mother's coming to kiss him good night.

Mais ce bonsoir durait si peu de temps, elle
redescendait si vite, que le moment où je
l'entendais monter . . . était pour moi un moment douloureux. Il *annonçait* celui qui allait
le suivre, où elle m'aurait quitté, où elle serait
redescendue. De sorte que ce bonsoir que j'ai-
mais tant, j'en arrivais à souhaiter qu'il vînt le
plus tard possible, à ce que se *prolongeât* le
temps de répit où maman n'était pas encore
venue. (I 13)

But this good night lasted for so short a time:
she went down again so soon that the moment
in which I heard her climb the stairs . . . was
for me a moment of keenest sorrow. It *an-
nounced* the moment to follow, when she
would have left me and gone back downstairs.
So much did I love that good night that I
reached the stage of hoping that it would come
as late as possible, so as to *prolong* the time of
respite during which Mamma would not yet
have appeared. (I 10)

The two verbs in italics designate the two complementary aspects of time: its action of forever
replacing one moment with another which extinguishes the last, the destructive aspect; and its action of sustaining certain moments by anticipation
or prolongation or recollection, its creative aspect.
Marcel remains pinioned between these two effects
of time until the closing pages. Then, in the middle
of the Prince de Guermantes' reception, he grasps
his dilemma as man and artist.

Mais une raison plus grave expliquait mon
angoisse; je découvrais cette action destructrice
du Temps au moment même où je voulais en-
treprendre de rendre claires, d'intellectualiser
dans une oeuvre d'art, des réalités extratempo-
relles (III 930)

But a still graver reason explained my distress;
I was discovering this destructive action of
Time at the very moment when I was about to
undertake to make clear and to intellectualise
in a literary work certain extratemporal realities.
(II 1038, revised)

What Marcel has watched but never recognized in the blurred, deflected experiences of many
years, now becomes the most naked and importunate presence in that crowded salon. Time, which
will soon destroy him, affords him the only op-
portunity to apply his "special sense" of life to a
work that will express the "extratemporal realities"
of memory and recognition. Marcel, lying in bed as
a child, could prolong his mother's good night for
a short time by his imaginative resourcefulness. But
Marcel, the writer, working desperately *against* time,
must strive to deliver these experiences from de-
struction into art.

What we find first then, looking back through
the novel at life, is this special sense that I have
dwelt on in terms of the optics of time. Particularly
we see it in Proust's stereoptican views of personality,
what he referred to in his interview with Elie-Joseph
Bois in *Le Temps* (12 Novembre 1913) as "not

plane psychology, but psychology in time." But (as Joseph Frank has suggested in a brilliant essay, "Spatial Form in Modern Literature," *The Sewanee Review*, 1945) when the principal characters are reassembled and displayed in an elaborate overlay of all the ages and actions at the end of the book, *time has become space*: we see it from a distance all at once. Proust himself now changes terms and describes his composition as "psychology in space" (III 1031/II 1111), a juxtaposition of all the contradictions and false scents of psychology in time.[8]

Because of the aptness of his terminology, Mr. Frank succeeds in describing succinctly the nature of Proust's esthetic as it is generally understood in reference to the *moments bienheureux*. "Proust's purpose is only achieved, therefore, when these units of meaning are referred to each other reflexively in a moment of time." Following a remark by Ramon Fernandez, he affirms that the essence of these momentary experiences is a "spatialization of time." The metaphor is instructive and relates to the stereoscopic principle already discussed: Proust arrests the flow of time by grasping it in certain related units, in *instantanés*. The first and doubtless best known example, is the enumeration in the opening pages of the rooms Marcel has lived in (I 6-8/I 5-7). These different places clearly represent different times as well, now held simultaneously in the mind. But quite apart from having overlooked the more fundamental experience of recognition, Mr. Frank, like most critics, has grievously missed the point. If we look back through the novel as a whole, and not just at the anthology pieces, we see something far different and more significant.

Except for a few fleeting revelations in the beginning, Marcel comes into full possession of this special sense of time only at the end of a long and almost abandoned quest. He has to penetrate a sequence of historical events along the false scents of temporal order before attaining the vision of pure time. It is not given but earned, achieved. A *la recherche* relates a journey, a progress which cannot be discounted just because it reaches its destination against all expectations. *There is no substitute for living, for the thickness of human time traversed.* Just here, Proust's prolonged narrative and oblique, flickering presentation of character resolve into a courageous personal morality rarely discerned: we must create our own character by living, by surviving the succession of errors which is our lot. When he comes to declare himself directly on life and art in one of the capital passages of the book, Proust significantly frames it by attributing it to the painter Elstir.

"Il n'y a pas d'homme si sage qu'il soit, me dit-il, qui n'ait à telle époque de sa jeunesse prononcé des paroles, ou même mené une vie, dont le souvenir lui soit désagréable et qu'il souhaiterait être aboli. Mais il ne doit pas absolument le regretter, parce qu'il ne peut être assuré d'être devenu un sage, dans la mesure où cela est possible, que s'il a passé par toutes les incarnations ridicules ou odieuses qui doivent précéder cette dernière incarnation-là. Je sais qu'il y a des jeunes gens, fils et petits-fils d'hommes distingués, à qui leurs précepteurs ont enseigné la noblesse de l'esprit et l'élégance morale dès le collège. Ils n'ont peut-être rien à retrancher de leur vie, ils pourraient publier et signer tout ce qu'ils ont dit, mais ce sont de pauvres esprits, descendants sans force de doctrinaires, et de qui la sagesse est négative et stérile. On ne reçoit pas la sagesse, il faut la découvrir soi-même après un trajet que personne ne peut faire pour nous, ne peut nous épargner, car elle est un point de vue sur les choses. Les vies que vous admirez, les attitudes que vous trouvez nobles n'ont pas été disposées par le père de famille ou par le précepteur, elles ont été précédées de débuts bien différents, ayant été influencées par ce qui régnait autour d'elles de mal ou de banalité. Elles représentent un combat et une victoire. Je comprends que l'image de ce que nous avons été dans une période première ne soit plus reconnaissable et soit en tous cas déplaisante. Elle ne doit pas être reniée pourtant, car elle est un témoignage que nous avons vraiment vécu, que c'est selon les lois de la vie et de l'esprit que nous avons, des éléments communs de la vie, de la vie des ateliers, des coteries artistiques s'il s'agit d'un peintre, extrait quelque chose qui les dépasse." (1864)

"There is no man," he began, "however wise, who has not at some period of his youth said things, or lived in a way the consciousness of which is so unpleasant to him in later life that he would gladly, if he could, expunge it from his memory. And yet he ought not entirely to regret it, because he cannot be certain that he has indeed become a wise man—so far as it is possible for any of us to be wise—unless he has passed through all the fatuous or unwholesome incarnations by which that ultimate stage must be preceded. I know that there are young fellows, the sons and grandsons of famous men, whose masters have instilled into them nobility of mind and moral refinement in their schooldays. They have, perhaps, when they look back upon their past lives, nothing to retract; they can, if they choose, publish a signed account of everything they have ever said or done; but they are poor creatures, feeble descendants of doctrinaires, and their wisdom is negative and sterile. We are not provided with wisdom, we must discover it for ourselves, after a journey through the wilderness which no one else can take for us, an effort which no one can spare us, for our wisdom is the point of view from which we come at last to regard the world. The lives that you admire, the attitudes that seem noble to you are not the result of training at home, by a father, or by masters at school, they have sprung from beginnings of a very different order, by reaction from the influence of everything evil or commonplace that prevailed round about them. They represent a struggle and a victory. I can see that the picture of what we once were, in early youth, may not be recognisable and cannot, certainly, be pleasing to contemplate in later life. But we must not deny the truth of it, for it is evidence that we have really lived, that it is in accordance with the laws of life and of the mind that we have, from the common elements of life, of the life of studios, of artistic groups—assuming that one is a painter—extracted something that goes beyond them." (1 649)

Read attentively in the light of the entire novel, this page needs little comment. It is as personal and as universal an affirmation of individual experience as Montaigne's superb essays, *Du repentir* and *De l'expérience*. Elstir tells Marcel (to whom it all means very little until much later, when he has learned for himself) that life cannot be dispensed with and cannot be taught; it must be lived. One has to find out for oneself, and what one comes to is a "point of view" on one's own experience. Here lies true wisdom. The victory may belong to an instant, but it cannot be attained without lengthy combat. In this code of self-reliance the novel reaches beyond any particular ethic or morality to assert a faith in the process of life as discovery.[9] We can now better understand Proust-Marcel's profound preoccupation with and reverence for age. A genuine prestige attaches to the mere fact of a person's having passed through a certain segment of time. This attitude forms one of many biblical elements in *A la recherche*.

I consider it significant that Tolstoy takes the same blunt attitude toward the irreducible, irreplaceable process of living. In the magnificent story, *Family Happiness*, Sergey finally explains to his wayward wife why he did not use his authority or persuasion to keep her from the temptation of worldly society.

> "Yes," he began, as if continuing his thoughts aloud, "all of us, and especially you women, must have personal experience of all the nonsense of life, in order to get back to life itself; the evidence of other people is no good."

And the reason why Pierre occupies the center of interest in *War and Peace*, gradually displacing Andrew and Natasha for all their allure, is that he pursues so many false scents. We feel the full force of his experience, his restlessness, and his impatience with shoddy answers. No one answers Pierre's mighty questions; he simply takes time to discover his being and assume himself.

Now, for all the rugged strength of this attitude toward life, it confronts us with a great dilemma regarding literature. Does it not seem that these two masters of the novel confound themselves by denying any final value to their own work? If we must learn through personal experience, following a progress of self-realization that cannot be hastened or influenced without some kind of damage to what we really are, what is the purpose of literature? Why read a book which, according to the deepest convictions of its author, we cannot sub-

stitute for life truly lived? The question is not spe-
cious. On the contrary, it probes toward the essential
nature of literary experience and artistic experience
in general. But I shall defer any attempt to answer
the question, both because the appropriate terms
will emerge later and because merely ruminating
over the question a while may induce better understanding of it.

What Marcel achieves or earns through living
in Proust's novel, the art found after a lifetime of
disappointments and missteps, comes clear to us as
readers but cannot serve us as it serves him. Proust-
Marcel's estheticism, or what some would call his
mysticism, grows in this world where we must
fend for ourselves. No matter how refined and tenu-
ous Proust's fabric may become, he never swerves
from a sense of "life as worthy of being lived"
(III 1032/II 1112).

> . . . cette réalité que nous risquerions fort de
> mourir sans avoir connue, et qui est tout sim-
> plement notre vie. La vraie vie, la vie enfin
> découverte et éclaircie, la seule vie par con-
> séquent réellement vécue, c'est la littérature;
> cette vie qui, en un sens, habite à chaque in-
> stant chez tous les hommes aussi bien que chez
> l'artiste. (III 895)

> . . . that reality which there is grave danger
> we might die without ever having known and
> yet which is simply our life, life as it really is,
> life disclosed at last and made clear, conse-
> quently the only life that is really lived, is

literature; that life which in one sense is to be
found at every moment in every man, as well
as in the artist. (II 1013, corrected)

We hear the strength of conviction that lodges in
the word, "literature," as Proust closes in on it. But
what follows, the little phrase, "in one sense," con-
cedes that this value cannot mean to all of us (in
spite of the statement) what it means to the author-
narrator.

It might be possible now to define A la recherche as the dramatization of a set of moral and
epistemological truths; but the weakest part of that
description is the word "dramatization." Marcel's
drama is so slow-paced, so extended and even at-
tenuated between beginning and end, that we can
use the word only in a restricted, nearly Oriental
sense of an inward drama expressed in a few highly
ritualized gestures. And the Oriental aspect of A la
recherche goes very deep. A multiplicity of images,
laws, and fleeting illuminations lie along the course
of our existence, but only a sustained and disci-
plined pursuit of ourselves inwardly, only life truly
lived leads to wisdom. One of the greatest achievements in the Western tradition of the novel, A la
recherche also joins the Oriental tradition of works
of meditation and initiation into the mysteries of
life. We can read as far into it as our age and understanding allow. A dedicated mondain in Paris for
half his life, Proust went on to probe far beyond the
culture that reared him, and far beyond Catholi-
cism, Judaism, and idealist philosophy. The poet

and Orientalist, René Daumal, provides a frame in which to see this achievement.

The Modern Man believes himself adult, a finished product, with nothing to do for the rest of his life but alternately earn and spend material things (money, vital forces, skills), without these exchanges having the slightest effect on the thing called "I." The Hindu regards himself as something still to be formed, a false vision to be corrected, a composite of substances to be transmuted, a multitude to be unified. . . .

Among us, men are considered equal in what they *are*, and different by what they *have*: innate qualities and acquired skills. The Hindu recognizes a hierarchy in men's degree of being. The master is not just more knowing or more clever than the student; the former *is*, in substance, more than the latter. This is what makes possible the unbroken transmission of the truth. (*Chaque fois que l'aube paraît*, p. 232-233)

In his intricate weaving of figures around the optics of time and in his emphasis on creating our own deliverance from time in the inwardness of life at every moment, Proust reveals his close kinship to Oriental thought and the traditional Oriental mood of life. Amid the bravura activism and possessiveness of the West—political, commercial, social, and sentimental—his novel assumes the proportions of a gospel. Proust had no use for "the poor in spirit," confident in their upbringing and inheritance. He wrote for those, including himself, who feel that the full meaning and value of life is ours to discover.

V

—◆—

The ambitiousness of Proust's undertaking, from its sheer length to its metaphysical aspirations, makes enormous demands on his literary style. It has survived countless attacks to become one of the best known, and least imitated, of all prose styles. As his novel tenaciously aims at assimilating the whole meaning of life, so each sentence strives to digest its whole subject, and a kind of elephantiasis sets in. But this retentive, monumental aspect of Proust's writing does not prevent it from being astonishingly flexible. With these apparently unwieldy sentences, he can, for example, braid together the multiple strands forming a social gathering and allow one after the other to come forward and retreat into the background, to form a thick tissue of intermixed conversations, multi-faceted characters, and fragmentary encounters. This rich prose fuses into a highly sensuous and simultaneous present within which the possible explanations and possible effects of any gesture mutiply to infinity. But the final effect is not exactly what one might anticipate, for one is finally reduced, by the very mass of writing itself, to a few tiny but indubitable facts: Odette addressed a letter to M. de Forcheville; La Berma took the role of Phèdre; Mme. de Guermantes wore red shoes; Albertine opened the window. Upon these slender foundations the action of the novel rests. Its incredible complexity arises out of this simplicity through the displacement, the divergence, the difference by which the human consciousness beholds the world.

The book's central metaphor, which arches over the entire action, interior and exterior, is contained in the *deux côtés*, a division of the environs of Combray and of the universe into two parts later reconciled and recognized as one. Yet it has never been pointed out that the *deux côtés* represent most basically the action of metaphor itself—different elements folding into one. Proust-Marcel lives a palpable metaphor that implants in the story itself "the links essential for good style" (III 889/II 1008-09) and that suggests by geography the gradual commingling of contrasting areas of consciousness. To grow up seems to bring to bear on the forces of life itself the reconciling and revelatory power known in literature as metaphor. Thus as Marcel reaches maturity the figure of the *deux côtés* comes to stand for the two controlling dualities in the action. The first duality is that of the two *snobismes* that fascinate Marcel as he grows up—the lure of the higher aristocratic levels of society and the lure of the basest, most vulgar and most depraved levels. He has little but scorn for anything in between. It is this double snobbery that causes Marcel's original indifference to Albertine (I 844/I 635) and arouses his desire for Baronne de Putbus' maid and for the well-born girl who frequents a *maison de passe*—when he has laid eyes on neither (II 723/II 89). Marcel has to acknowledge the aptness of M. de Charlus' terse metaphor for this social attitude: "Pas de milieu. *Phèdre* or *Les Saltimbanques*" (III 830/II 965).

The second duality consists of the two paths of knowledge that for years determine Marcel's response to any event or sensation. What he has experienced seems inevitably trivial, whereas all the mystery and promise of life appear to lie in a higher realm not yet explored. After Marcel has met the well-born Mme. de Villeparisis and received a poor impression (because, among other things, she likes oysters), his grandmother suggests that the aged lady may be related to the Guermantes, most aristocratic of families, none of whom Marcel has yet met. He reacts immediately and in terms of the duality that still holds him in thrall.

Comment aurais-je pu croire à une communauté d'origine entre deux noms qui étaient entrés en moi, l'un par la porte basse et honteuse de l'expérience, l'autre par la porte d'or de l'imagination. (I 698)

How could I be expected to believe in a common origin uniting two names which had entered my consciousness, one through the low and shameful gate of experience, the other by the golden gate of imagination? (1 529)

The familiar and the unknown seem to represent opposite poles of experience. The immense geographical polarity of the *deux côtés*, which turns out to be an optical illusion of childhood, subsumes both these moral polarities, though the correspondence is nowhere explicitly made. Just as the two different "ways" of the landscape in Combray finally disappear when Marcel later visits Gilberte at Tansonville, and particularly when he beholds Mlle. de Saint-Loup approaching him in the final recognition of his own life, so the two *snobismes* and the two ways of experience fuse into one in the final pages. In Mlle. de Saint-Loup, symbolizing the mongrel composition of the entire salon, the blood of a *cocotte* notorious for the dimensions of her shoddy past mingles with the best blood of the aristocracy; the irreconcilable opposites which attracted Marcel to princesses and milk maids have flowed into one.

This meeting also resolves Marcel's deep moral conflict over the two "gates" of knowledge. For years he has been paralyzed by the opposite attractions of society and solitude, worldly experience and inward sensibility. Each of the two paths has led him astray. In society, he ends up as bored with the Guermantes' tedious dinners as with the Verdurins' pretentious soirées. In solitude he miscalculates his own true feelings as grievously as he does Gilberte's or Albertine's. The reconciliation of these two paths of knowledge takes the shape of the work of art, an outward act representing an inward state of mind. In the final scene Marcel no longer needs to flee the mustered forces of Paris society in order to find inner peace and self-recognition. The faces have ceased being distractions and have become revelations. As anticipated by Elstir's sturdy morality of living and learning for oneself, Marcel now knows where he is and who he is. He recognizes both his milieu and himself in the same spectacular scene, and that complementary recognition releases him from his dilemma. He can now produce a work of art, the narrative of his personal experience. In the very words of the novel we are reading, the *deux côtés* of experience have become one.

The action which dominates all of A *la recherche*, then, is the action of metaphor: the reconciliation of a duality or, in more complex cases, of a multiplicity. It encompasses all aspects of the book, from the aspects of personality to the division of society itself to the stereoscopic assembling of past and present. Marcel finally understands that he has himself produced this great fusion by growing up, by coming to terms with himself, by living his own life as no one else could live it for him, and by heeding the vocation of literature. The circle of this vast metaphor closes only in the last two hundred pages and is soldered by the final apparition of Mlle. de Saint-Loup barely fifteen pages before the end. And just here I have my principal criticism to make of the book as Proust left it—enlarged, strengthened, monumental, faithful to his original conception. This total reorientation of the action, embodied in the transformation of Marcel's life in the final pages, demands some corresponding elevation in style to lift us out of the level established by twenty-six hundred pages of prose. Not that Proust's prose has been monotonous, quite the contrary. He has unlimbered so much of his arsenal that one feels he has no reserves left to throw into this final passage. Proust, hypnotized by his own sentence structure, cannot now abandon his elaborate syntax and exhaustive analysis of inward states simply to write a poem. For the action demands a stylistic departure as radical as that. And the fact is, as Feuillerat points out, that Proust has been preparing this *coup de théâtre* for so many pages and so many years, has (perhaps out of a fear of not completing the final scene as he wanted it) anticipated the final revelation so many times, that much of the dramatic effect of the end is vitiated. We can see it coming. The close of the novel remains one of the most magnificent achievements in all fiction, but had Proust lived to comb back through the entire novel and remove some of the passages where he forgets the esthetic of the false scent and tells us too much, the shock of recognition would have been even greater at the end.

The one clear stylistic indication that Proust tried to lift this whole final sequence to a higher level of discourse, to thrust it almost physically *hors du temps*, lies in his frequent introduction of imagery of altitude. This is not one of Stendhal's ambitious heroes dominating the world but Marcel finally dominating time and the vast dimensions of his own life. On his way to the prince's *matinée*, Marcel's carriage suddenly rolls along easily as it comes out onto the smooth pavement of the Champs-Elysées. The effect of release is strong and immediate.

> Et, comme un aviateur qui a jusque-là péniblement roulé à terre, "décollant" brusquement, je m'élevais lentement vers les hauteurs silencieuses du souvenir. (III 858)

> And, like an aviator who has been laboriously rolling along the ground and then suddenly takes off, I rose slowly toward the silent heights of memories past. (II 956)

On its next appearance, the altitude figure clearly refers to the dedicated life of art.

> J'avais vécu comme un peintre montant un chemin qui surplombe un lac dont un rideau de rochers et d'arbres lui cache la vue. (III 1035)

> I had lived like a painter climbing a road overlooking a lake, which is hidden from his eyes by a curtain of rocks and trees. (II 1114)

And then it is Marcel, perched atop the mountain of his own life, precarious and triumphant.

J'éprouvais un sentiment de fatigue et d'effroi
à sentir que tout ce temps si long non seulement avait, sans une interruption, été vécu,
pensé, sécrété par moi, qu'il était ma vie, qu'il
était moi-même, mais encore que j'avais à toute
minute à le maintenir attaché à moi, qu'il me
supportait, moi, juché à son sommet vertigi-
neux, que je ne pouvais me mouvoir sans le
déplacer. (III 1047)

There came over me a feeling of profound
fatigue at the realisation that all this long
stretch of time not only had been uninter-
ruptedly lived, thought, secreted by me, that it
was my life, my very self, but also that I must,
every minute of my life, keep it closely by me,
that it upheld me, that I was perched on its
dizzying summit, that I could not move without carrying it about with me. (II 1123)

On the next page—the last—Proust borrows the
figure Montaigne employs in the closing paragraph
of his last essay to ridicule men's overweening aspirations to divinity and immortality. But Proust is
essentially serious when he paints Marcel as a man
on "living stilts," and then as a giant, plunged into
and rising out of Time. All these figures of altitude
are in reality images for an extended and deepened
vision. Altitude represents the capacity to see far,
to bring together and combine in the mind's eye
images enormously removed from one another. The
magic lantern which transforms Marcel's room in
the opening pages metamorphoses at the end into

the stereoscopic vision of a giant standing erect in life and thus commanding Time.[10]

The imposing scale of Proust's undertaking and the extent to which he accomplished it keep our attention directed toward the unfolding of the action itself rather than toward the multiple extraneous questions which often distract us from a work of literature. But one is perfectly justified in asking if there are any parallels to this work, any other major works to which it is related by anything from plagiarism to archetypical participation. We are as accustomed in the twentieth century as were medieval commentators to link great contemporary texts to ancient forebears; thus Joyce resurrects the *Odyssey* and Faulkner the Christ story and Mann the Joseph story, and every playwright worth his salt has raided Aeschylus and Sophocles. Even though Proust's work abounds in semi-mythical themes like magical initiation and fetishism, and though it extends the highly conscious tradition of the literary memoir, he wrote what impresses one as essentially a self-contained novel. *A la recherche* relies upon no exterior counterpart to sustain or reflect its action; on the contrary Proust set about to create within the massive dimensions of his work the very parallels which would illuminate its meaning. The novel contains its own past in the form of incidents forgotten and then recalled under special circumstances. The story resurrects only itself. In contrast to the linear progression of a fairy story which immediately reveals its features in the opening formula: *Once upon a time . . .* , Proust follows a compound rhythm of expression which might be partly conveyed in the expression: *Twice upon a time.* Within the limits of the novel Proust creates a form of double consciousness, which I have examined at length as stereologic or binocular vision in time. As our two pupils, when properly functioning, form one three-dimensional image in the mind, so the experience of two related events separated and connected by the proper interval of *oubli* forms one four-dimensional image in the consciousness—a *moment bienheureux* when it occurs fleetingly and without lasting effect on our life pattern, a self-recognition and piercing of the veil of illusion when we are able to sustain our consciousness at this level.

In an exceptionally illuminating page of *Le Mythe de Sisyphe*, Camus asserts this double consciousness as a central principle. "To create is to live twice. The anxious groping search of a man like Proust, his meticulous collecting of flowers and tapestries and states of anguish has no other meaning" (p. 130). The basic action of the book is intermittent and constantly in decline until the close; the occasional references to a former life and to metempsychosis should be read figuratively as signifying levels of our own existence, the multiplicity of our states of awareness which we tend to spread out successively in time. Achieving its deepest insights and formal beauties by returning to and surpassing itself, *A la recherche* must be seen as reflexive in shape, a narrative which turns back upon itself and rises out of itself in a spiral.

This essential self-containment of Proust's novel by no means prevents its significance from joining human experience. The conjunction takes place, however, at a very deep level. Valéry isolated an aspect of this intersection of meaning when he spoke of how Proust makes us vividly aware of the *infini en puissance* of the process of life, that is, the infinite range of possibilities that circle us at every moment and that any act or event—the sheer enactment of every present moment—fatefully reduces to a single strand. Before this dwindling of the opulent promise of the future into the paltry past, we feel a profound anxiety and disenchantment. But—and here Valéry has grasped only the first part of Proust's novel—*A la recherche* brings a reversal of this process of impoverishment. The double consciousness of recognition and re-creation heightens and strengthens our life to the point where it is no longer subject to the erosion of time's flow.

Armed now with this sense of double consciousness in time, of living twice, we are ready to approach the question that has gone many pages unanswered. Why, when only personal experience, only life itself can bring us to ourselves and to any kind of fulfilment, why do we have literature? The most stalwart of writers, among them Proust and Tolstoy, affirm that literature cannot ever be a substitute for experience. But—and here is the point—it is not therefore excluded from any role in shaping our experience.

Literature, as one among the arts, acquaints us with a special and intensified repertory of feelings and events and possibilities. Later when we come upon an event, we may have a counterpart already at hand, forgotten, but available. And the movement of our mind is to say: "This is it." For we have lived it once already.

Literature can foreshorten the complex, two-part process of full living; what we participate in through reading becomes the first half of that double process. Our own life, our personal experience, can then move directly into the second beat: recognition.

The action I am trying to describe resembles the elaborate training pilots were put through in the Second World War in order to be able to recognize instantaneously all enemy aircraft. In a flash lasting one hundredth of a second, a pilot could know, "That's a Zero." He could not be taught exactly how to bag the Japanese plane when he met one; but he could be taught, through this preparation, to concentrate all his powers on the task when the time came. Similarly, to read genuine literature is to accumulate within oneself a fund of possible experiences against which to achieve an occasionally intensified sense of what one is doing, to recognize that one is alive in a particular way. I remember the verb to "Proustify" that I traded with classmates in college when we first explored Proust's novel. The word referred to a certain kind of urgent, involuntary recollection that we all experienced from time to time and that now took on crucial significance because we had read Proust and accepted this experience as something no longer trivial. We were constantly on the alert with our inner spectroscopes. Literature, then, like all the arts, plays a formative or preparatory role in training our sensibilities. In a limited way it supplies the first beat of a duple rhythm of existence. It offers not true life, but the potentiality of true life if we go on to complete that rhythm. *A la recherche* and *War and Peace* do not represent the wasted effort of authors who can offer us no more than skillful diversion. As Proust's optical figures insist, true literature does not divert but directs. The great books affect the economy of life for many individuals by allowing them to achieve personal experience sooner, more directly, and with less groping. This sense, this secret, is what allows certain people to live life at all times as an adventure. Others simply do not recognize that what they are doing, what is going on around them, has any significance as *life* at all. Literature is one of the keys.

This apparently simplistic explanation of the experience of literature holds up even in reverse. The person who has lived a full, varied life frequently fails to recognize its meaning or even to appreciate its qualities until encountering it afresh in a work of art—particularly literature. (In all this section "literature" must be read in the broad sense of any compelling account of experience—fireside story or epic, poem, biography, or lyric phrase.) Whereas the young—in almost the optical sense— look forward to life through literature, the old look back at life through it. In both cases a metamorphosis occurs if the process finds its second term—either the event re-encountered in the future after an interval of forgetting, or the event rediscovered in the past before it was forgotten. Thus Proust could speak of a reader as reading into his own self. (III 911/II 1024).

This second experience commonly occurs accompanied by mixed feelings over having to acknowledge: "Yes, it was just like that and I never knew it." Roquentin in Sartre's *Nausea* looks back in amazement as he works on a biography and realizes that he has seen more of the world and of life than most people. The second beat of life comes to him after the living, and his "adventures" are discovered in restrospect until the terror of nausea plunges him into something more urgent. But I cannot help feeling that the reverse order of events leads to the more authentic experience: literature establishes the terms in which later events will be met. Literature itself contains a host of illustrations of this process—Paolo and Francesca reading romances together, Don Quixote reading tales of chivalry, Julien Sorel reading Napoleon, Emma Bovary reading novels, Tom Sawyer reading pirate stories. The precise equilibrium of forces between life and literature is one of literature's major themes. Proust makes it particularly urgent by the massive steadiness with which his novel directs our attention back at ourselves. On what level, in what rhythm, with what intensity are we alive?

Even though the relationship of *A la recherche* to the Western literary tradition is different from that of such masters as Balzac or Hardy or even Dostoevsky, there still remain a certain number of comparisons which shed light on Proust's novel. Homer, for example, puts off Ulysses' homecoming almost to the point of his (and our) forgetting it— but never completely; then the long prepared return takes place in an elaborate series of disguises, unmaskings, and recognitions not unlike the close of Proust's novel. Long wandering followed by a homecoming—few actions are more universal. French literature itself produced the three writers whose work turns most compulsively and searchingly back upon itself in order to find out the charm and the mystery of the past. Montaigne, Rousseau, and Chateaubriand strove to discover themselves as men and as writers through works of memory and reflection that engulf all their other writings. But the essay, the confession, and the memoir each faces in a different direction from the novel. More than any other modern novelist, Tolstoy in *War and Peace* conveys a sense of people's aging, losing and gaining in knowledge, circling around their own image of themselves. But where Tolstoy relied increasingly on a sense of family and progeny as the continuity of life, Proust held his universe tightly arrayed around one individual consciousness.

It is a slightly wider meaning of literary tradition that must accommodate itself to Proust's work: the tradition of legends and folk tales we usually devour in our childhood. *A la recherche* is closer to *Arabian Nights* than any other work. In his final meditation on the literary vocation and death, Marcel speculates that his book will demand many nights of work, perhaps a thousand. And then *A Thousand and One Nights* (along with Saint-Simon's memoirs) quietly appears to give its blessing to these closing pages (III 1043-1044/ II 1120-21). Of course, Proust-Marcel states that his book will be quite different. But the differences take root in several significant similarities. Both stories begin by presenting a secure and happy life soon shattered by a revelation of infidelity and depravity. The Sultan discovers his wife is deceiving him on a grand scale, and his eyes are opened to the unfaithfulness of all women. Marcel's innocent vision of Combray collapses beneath the weight of vice and duplicity that reveal themselves in every character outside his immediate family. Thus set adrift in a corrupt world, both stories move in apparently desultory fashion through magic powers, evil presence, cryptic events, and transformations in people. In the long middle reaches, everyone seems to be reduced to "passing time." But the beginning and end of the action stay firmly in place in the two books. The narrative, Marcel's or Scheherezade's, is carried on in defiance of fate and time, and so great persistence wins release and salvation for the two story tellers. Thus literature wins out day by day over death. Scheherezade gains pardon for herself and coaxes the Sultan back to humanity of feeling by bringing to him the three children he has begotten during the thousand nights she has been his companion. Proust employs a similar incarnation of time lived in Mlle. de Saint-Loup, the figure in whom Marcel finally recognizes himself and becomes reconciled to his world and his vocation. The parallels between the two stories are more than casual. I am inclined to think Proust took pleasure in considering himself, despite disclaimers, as the author of *Parisian Nights*.

An equally illuminating comparison, this one apparently unfamiliar to Proust, can be made with a story taken from the folklore of the "New World." No tale is at the same time so entrancing and so disturbing as that of the long sleep of the hunter who loses twenty years of his life in the depths of the Catskills, as Marcel loses long years in his *maisons de santé*. The real sleep of Rip Van Winkle confronts him, when he returns to his village, with a foreshortening of time and a scene of recognitions like the one at the close of *A la recherche*. Time, however, has bested Rip, passed him by and left him with nothing more than "his place on the bench at the inn door" and a good tale to tell any traveler who will listen to a garrulous old man. Marcel's literary sleep, on the other hand, has the opposite effect. It allows him to best time, to rise out of contingency. For it bestows on him at last and for good the sense of *la vraie vie* which he only grazed earlier in the *moments bienheureux* and in the twilight consciousness on the edge of sleep. Marcel's long forgetting does not remain a mere pathetic curiosity of local legend like Rip's, but permits him the stereoscopic vision of time, the double consciousness of existence which gives *A la recherche* its shape and its meaning. Rip's long sleep and Marcel's disappearance amount to a death in life from which they return; our reward lies not in heaven but on earth insofar as we can resurrect ourselves from the death we face every moment.

NOTES

—◆—

1. More has been written about Proust in many languages than about any other author of the twentieth century. Yet few works in this gigantic bibliography of over three thousand items advance beyond the stage of assembling materials for an ultimate understanding of his work. The books which begin to probe into the quick are Pierre Abraham, *Proust* (Paris, 1930); Samuel Beckett, *Proust* (London, 1931; New York, Grove Press, n.d.); Germaine Brée, *Du temps perdu au temps retrouvé* (Paris, 1950; in English: New Brunswick, Rutgers, 1955); and most recently, Howard Moss, *The Magic Lantern of Marcel Proust*, New York, Macmillan, 1962. Useful introductions have been written or edited by Richard H. Barker, René Girard, Léon Guichard, Milton Hindus, Harold March, André Maurois, Léon Pierre-Quint, and Edmund Wilson.

It should be worth examining what Proust's

opponents have said, for the enemy often perceives a position better than the defending army. But here too we are disappointed; almost every attack has been made on an outlying position. Julien Benda's *La France byzantine* makes fascinating reading, as well as parts of Wyndham Lewis' *Time and Western Man*. But neither succeeds in engaging the full array of Proust's forces.

I should also mention an impressive yet exasperating work on Proust that provides one of the best reflectors into his universe. Albert Feuillerat's *Comment Marcel Proust a composé son roman* (New Haven, 1934) obliges us to acknowledge two versions of *A la recherche du temps perdu*: the three volumes Proust originally sought to publish in 1912, and the seven volumes (tripled in total length) to which it swelled in the ten years before Proust's death. Feuillerat makes a strong but not impervious case for the superior construction and greater purity of sensibility in the first version. Therefore I should make it clear here that I am dealing with Proust's novel in its entirety, in its hypertrophy—without, however, shrinking from an awareness and even the feel of the other version within, like a woman's body beneath her clothes.

The seven volumes (today bound again as three) represent neither a betrayal of the original beauty nor an elaborate camouflage of simplicity. One of the motives which caused me to undertake this study of Proust's novel is the conviction that its length results from a true growth in structure and sensibility. Like any aged tree, the work shows unhealed wounds, distorted limbs, and parasitic growth. But they cannot stifle its vigor.

The only perceptive texts on Proust's images are recent: Reino Virtanen, "Proust's Metaphors from the Natural and Exact Sciences," *PMLA*, December 1954; and Stephen Ullman, *The Image in the Modern French Novel* (Chapter III, "The Metaphorical Texture of a Proustian Novel"), Cambridge, 1960. The first of these texts supplies detailed illustration of my remarks in these opening pages and has allowed me to condense my exposition.

2. Page references are to the following editions: *A la recherche du temps perdu*, NRF, Bibliothèque de la Pléiade, 3 t., 1955, and *Remembrance of Things Past*, translated by C. K. Scott Moncrieff and Frederick A. Blossom, Random House, 2 vols., 1934. Copyrighted and reprinted by permission of Editions Gallimard and Random House. Minor corrections have occasionally been made in the translation to conform to the revised French edition and to modify some interpretations. *In text* quotations are given in my own translation, followed by references to the Pléiade and Random House editions. A line (e.g. III 980/——) means the passage was not included in the text translated by Moncrieff.

3. Here is a note that some may wish to pass over. I shall supply a few supplementary observations about optics—about light and space, about the human eye, about previous uses of optical imagery in art, and about Proust's familiarity with

optical science. Optics as an independent discipline has tended to lose its identity under the shadow of astronomy, atomic physics, and the theory of relativity. But the unity of optics as a field and a mode of thinking is too great to abandon.

Light is the most rapid and miraculous means we know by which one part of the universe can impinge on another across space. We know its behavior, but are less sure of its composition and means of propagation. At the same time light is one of the familiar elements of our environment; specifically, it is the most regularly changing condition we experience and therefore the basic source of our sense and measurement of time. Shifts in lighting yield hours and days, seasons and years. Rays of light can be refracted or reflected into an image of their source; thus optical instruments, the eye as well as those constructed by man, become our primary source of information on near and remote objects. In science the speed of light, having been accurately measured, has become an important and useful physical constant, with the unique advantage that it does not vary with the motion of its source or on the part of the observer. The science of optics has been deeply involved in all modern advances in the fields of electro-magnetism, quantum mechanics, and relativity. Light is the most important single factor in our knowledge of the universe. Yet, as is clear on every page of Proust, this medium of observation ultimately becomes a barrier to final knowledge. Light incorporates the limits of its own revelations. Heisenberg's indeterminacy principle affirms that in the observation of infinitesimally small phenomena, the very light energy by which we see them affects their velocity. And the light by which we observe distant heavenly bodies arises out of a vast expenditure of energy which, by the time their light has reached us millions of years later, may have led to the total modification or disintegration of those bodies. Such technical terms as "light years," "red giants," and "white dwarfs" take on an almost metaphysical meaning. Light then is the source of our truth and our error—and equally of our poetry.

The eye, which registers light for us, has characteristics which we ordinarily forget or take for granted. In its relaxed state the lens of the eye focuses on infinity, and it requires muscular tension to accommodate it to close vision of our immediate environment. With increasing age, our ability to accommodate declines, producing the state of presbyopia, the farsightedness of old men. Similarly only darkness can relax the iris, for light causes an immediate contraction of its aperture. All the finest adjustments of the eye are reflex; only the gross actions of opening and directing the eye fall under predominantly voluntary control. And when our vision has adjusted itself to an object, the accurate interpretation of its inverted image in our eye depends upon habit, memory, and attention. The optical image disappears entirely into consciousness and life process. Finally, even though all the events of vision occur in the few inches of tissue between the eye and occipital lobe at the back of our head, we see objects incontrovertibly *out there*, reassembled in space. Our principal knowledge of the third dimension of space results not from the exactness of the two dimensional images of it which we receive, but from the disagreement between the two different versions of space which reach our consciousness from two separated eyes. The binocular nature of human vision (which requires that we see double and cross-eyed) introduces into the seat of our consciousness the principle of essential discrepancy, of meaningful error. This illusion of relief in three dimensions would scarcely suffice if we could not move through space and explore the nature of that error in order to make sense of it.

It would be worse than foolish to try to trace the role of optical imagery in art. It is universal. One of the most ancient and haunting symbols of the magic of vision is the single schematic eye which pervades Egyptian art, both in the eternal profile of figure drawing and in haughty isolation on one side of many sarcophagi. Resuming the researches of late Greek painting, it was the Renaissance with its science of Albertian perspective that established optics as the central discipline of art. It becomes not only the method but the matter of Uccello's studies and paintings, and of Piranesi's drawings. This rational construction of space was not to be systematically broken down until the nineteenth century, when an optical revolution of new instruments and new theories of color and light provided expressive technique for the restlessness of modern sensibility. It was then that Impressionism, like the nineteenth-century novel, developed an art of instantaneous fragments, not of eternal poses.

Now I am not trying to suggest that all these significant aspects of optics were consciously present in Proust's mind as he came to compose his novel. But we must not forget that the science of optics, under its own name and without the fancy dress of relativity theory and wave mechanics, played a dominant role in the scientific advances of the period. It was during the last three decades of the nineteenth century and the opening of the twentieth, exactly coincident with Proust's career, that Helmholtz fully described the physiology of the eye; that Edison (see II 730) invented the incandescent lamp; that Abbe and Schott perfected optical glass; that Maxwell established the relationship of light and electricity; that Michelson and Morley performed their masterful experiment to test the ether; that the great mathematician Henri Poincaré, a friend and colleague of Bergson, was lecturing at the University of Paris on celestial mechanics and geometric optics (Proust mentions him twice in A *la recherche*); that the Lumière brothers invented the *cinématographe*, which replaced Edison's kinetescope (and it will remain a mystery how Proust missed exploiting the magic name of Lumière); that the magic lantern, the stereoscope, and the kaleidoscope had their greatest vogue; and that illumination of public buildings was first tried out on the Eiffel Tower for the Exposition of 1889. At the end of the nineteenth century the optician's shop in every French town offered a display of optical instruments and toys which constituted the most advanced collection of scientific devices in the community. Even the pharmacies could not rival this exoticism. Marcel refers four times to the *opticien* in Combray, to the exact location of his shop and to the contents of his window. And in the closing pages of the novel he compares himself as writer to the optician with his magnifying glass (III 1033/II 1113). Proust studied optics as a part of his physics course at the Lycée Condorcet in the eighties; he knew the *romans d'anticipation* of Jules Verne and the literate science fiction of Villiers de l'Isle-Adam, who wrote about Edison as "the sorcerer of Menlo Park." Like many others, Proust collected photographs of all his friends and studied them as new revelations of character. Optics figured in Proust's environment as nuclear physics and rocketry figure in ours, and he sensed its symbolic significance. With the exception of acoustics, which, with its derivatives of music and the inflections of the human voice, yields the next most important corpus of images in Proust's work, optics is the only discipline which spans the fields of physics, physiology, psychology, and esthetics. By being "celestial" as well, it lent itself to the tremendous demands Proust made of his material. In the long passage quoted on pages 13 to 15, it is this perspective of "human astronomy" that allows Proust to write: ". . . what we have forgotten that we ever said, or indeed what we never did say, flies to provoke hilarity even in another planet."

When the critic Vettard wrote an article com-

paring Proust and Einstein as "analytical vision-
aries" with an intuitive understanding of the great
natural laws (*NRF*, août 1922), Proust stated with
enthusiasm that he "found the article accurate"
(*Lettres à la NRF*, p. 259). Literally from his death-
bed he wrote Vettard one of the most revealing of
all his letters on his artistic intentions, a letter de-
veloping the microscope-telescope comparison already incorporated into his novel (III 1041/II 1118).
Considering the numerous and familiar applications
of the science, and the aptness of its laws and terminology to describe artistic processes and human
perception, it is not surprising that optics became
the controlling metaphor of Proust's fiction.

4. Medical research into brain functioning cor-
roborates these theories. Proust scholars should
read Dr. Wilder Penfield's report, "Some Mech-
anisms of Consciousness Discovered during Elec-
trical Stimulation of the Brain" (*Proceedings of
the National Academy of Sciences, January* 1958).
This eminent neurosurgeon demonstrates the existence of "a permanent record of the stream of
consciousness" in an unmapped area of the brain,
which he names the "interpretive cortex."

No man can recall by voluntary effort such a
wealth of detail. . . . Many a patient has told
me that the experience brought back by the
electrode is much more real than remembering. . . .
In addition to the experential flash-backs,
there is one other type of response . . . When
the electrode is applied, the patient has a sud-

den "feeling" about the present situation. . . .
It is a signal, for example, that the present
situation is familiar, that it has been experienced before. Or it is strange, perhaps.

Dr. Penfield suggests that this interpretive cortex
functions in situations like the recognition of a
friend after long absence. It is all there.

5. Leonardo da Vinci, in one brief note, touched
on all the relations in question here between time,
optics, and memory:

> Our judgment does not reckon in their
> exact and proper order things which have come
> to pass at different periods of time; for many
> things which happened many years ago will
> seem nearly related to the present, and many
> things that are recent will seem ancient, extend-
> ing back to the far-off period of our youth.
> And so it is with the eye, with regard to distant
> things, which when illuminated by the sun
> seem near to the eye, while many things which
> are near seem far off. (*The Notebooks of
> Leonardo da Vinci*, translated by Edward Mac-
> Curdy, Braziller, New York, 1947, vol. I, p. 67)

6. The most careful study of Proust's chronology
can be found in H. R. Jauss, *Zeit und Erinnerung
in Marcel Proust's "A la recherche du temps perdu,"*
Heidelberg, 1955. See also Appendix D in Pamela
Hansford Johnson, *Proust Recaptured*, Chicago
University Press, 1958.

7. Two other critics systematically list the
moments bienheureux and come up with different

totals from mine. Samuel Beckett (*Proust*, p. 23)
counts eleven *"fetiches,"* corresponding to my I-V,
VIII, and XI a-e, and he mentions a few others as
incomplete. Howard Moss (*The Magic Lantern
of Marcel Proust*, pp. 98-99) counts eighteen
"mnemonic resurrections," twelve of which correspond to twelve of mine, plus six different incidents.
The exact number is of no great importance but
makes an interesting comparison.

8. I shall avoid any judgment of whether
Proust's monumental yet perpetually self-correcting
psychology is "true." Like all psychologies it cannot
be either true or false but only self-consistent, like
Booleian or Minkowskian geometry; in the brilliance
of its conception, it serves as a corrective to our
conventional reliance on types and tendencies.
Proust's construction of character is a little like
those wonders of the world, the Pyramids, which,
by their very structure, are at the same time unin-
habitable and indestructible.

It will be evident that I reject the widely held
opinion that Proust systematically effects a crum-
bling or shredding [*émiettement*] of the personality,
to a point where it loses all identity. Quite the contrary, in A *la recherche* we are shown the mass of
raw materials out of which the contingencies of
life normally force us to manufacture personality—
for ourselves and for others. That process requires
a certain remove or distance from the subject, a
perspective which in the case of Marcel is supplied
only in the briefest of *instantanés* until the end.
Sartre (who tried over and over to "escape from"

Proust) refers pertinently to him in one of his discussions of the "facticity" of character: "Proust's hero 'has no' character that can be directly grasped" (*L'Etre et le néant*, p. 416). Exactly. Insofar as we identify with Marcel, we live inside him where one is aware of no "personality" or "character." It is almost like finding oneself in the eye of a typhoon, where there seems to be no storm. The *recul* or distance that reveals personality, as it brings on the violence of a typhoon, comes only for a few pages at the end of Proust's novel. Otherwise we experience Marcel as a series of inconglomerate thought processes.

There is considerable pertinence in the comparison of Proust's treatment of character to the technique of divisionism. In this brand of impressionist painting we learn to reassemble the parts into a vibrant whole that we recognize anew. The process is particularly difficult, of course, when applied to oneself. The critic who has written perceptively about the close relation of self-recognition and personality in Proust is Georges Poulet in *Studies in Human Time*.

9. Some ten years earlier in his lengthy introduction (1906) to Ruskin's *Sésame et les lys* Proust made a preliminary statement.

Mais par une loi singulière et d'ailleurs providentielle de l'optique des esprits (loi qui signifie peut-être que nous ne pouvons recevoir la vérité de personne, et que nous devons la créer nous-même), ce qui est le terme de leur

sagesse ne nous apparaît que comme le com-
mencement de la nôtre, de sorte que c'est au
moment où ils nous ont dit tout ce qu'ils
pouvaient nous dire qu'ils font naître en nous
le sentiment qu'ils ne nous ont encore rien dit.
(pp. 32-33)

But by a singular and moreover providential
law of minds (a law that possibly signifies
that we can receive the truth from no one else
and must create it ourselves), the final achievement of their wisdom appears to us as only the
beginning of our own, so that it is just when
they have told us everything they can that they
awake in us the feeling that they haven't yet
said a thing.

These two statements about each man forging the
truth for himself, since they describe the deepest
moral tone of the novel, lead me to object strenu-
ously to an otherwise convincing article by Robert
Champigny on Proust, Bergson, and Kierkegaard
(*PMLA*, March 1957; reprinted in *Proust*, René
Girard, editor, Prentice Hall, 1962). Professor
Champigny maintains that "the man of Proust
can create, but cannot create himself." He discovers
in Proust a passive surrender to the instant. Everything I have said should refute this interpretation.
Marcel achieves, before all, a self-creation to which
the novel bears constant witness.

10. I cannot resist quoting from a standard text-
book on optics a paragraph which repeats this same
figure and summarizes all the optical effects I have

discussed earlier in relation to Proust's metaphors and methods.

"These stereoscopic photographs with enhanced relief were exceedingly useful during the war in locating gun emplacements, which, although skillfully camouflaged necessarily extended for several feet above the ground. In the stereoscope, the exaggeration of the depth dimension caused these emplacements to become conspicuous. In other words, the scene in the stereoscope appeared to the observer exactly as the original scene would have appeared to a giant with an interpupillary distance equal to the stereoscopic base." (Arthur C. Hardy and Fred H. Perrin, *The Principles of Optics*, McGraw-Hill, New York, 1932, p. 528)

Note: Several months after this book appeared, Georges Poulet published *L'Espace Proustien* (NRF, 1963). Some of his thinking about *lieu, distance, jonction,* and *juxtaposition* so closely parallels my own (for which I employ the terms *image, oubli,* cinematographic principle, and montage principle) that I regard his book as a kind of confirmation. His comments stop short of examining the stereoscopic principle, which I continue to consider essential. In a magnificent appendix, he assembles the evidence about a physiological-psychological occurrence all the rest of us had overlooked: the panoramic vision or total recall of a person on the point of death.

R. S.

May 1966